IF YOU LOVE ME

*Serving Christ and the Church
in Spirit and Truth*

MATTHEW THE POOR

TRANSLATED BY JAMES HELMY

ANCIENT FAITH PUBLISHING
CHESTERTON, INDIANA

If You Love Me: Serving Christ and the Church in Spirit and Truth
English translation copyright © James Helmy

Originally published in Arabic as *El-khedma* by the Monastery of St.
Macarius the Great, Wadi el-Natrun (Egypt), 1980. Translation published
by permission.

Published by:
  Ancient Faith Publishing
  A Division of Ancient Faith Ministries
  P.O. Box 748
  Chesterton, IN 46304

Unless otherwise noted, Scripture quotations are taken from the New
King James Version, © 1979, 1980, 1982 by Thomas Nelson, Inc. Used by
permission.

ISBN: 978-1-944967-32-1

Printed in the United States of America

25 24 23 22 21 20 19   16 15 14 13 12 11 10 9 8 7 6 5 4 3

For Dora—JH

Contents

Preface

5

Introduction

9

PART ONE

The Nature of Christian Service

15

CHAPTER 1

Love: The Ultimate Criterion of Christian Service

17

CHAPTER 2

Qualities of the Christian Servant

19

CHAPTER 3

The Essence of Christian Service

29

CHAPTER 4

Those We Serve

37

CHAPTER 5

Diseases of the Flock

39

CHAPTER 6

The Edification of the Christian Servant

47

CHAPTER 7

Stumbling Blocks for the Christian Servant

65

CHAPTER 8

The Mandatory "Taxes" Paid by the Christian Servant

87

CHAPTER 9

The Joys of the Christian Servant

93

PART TWO

On the Education of the Christian Servant

101

CHAPTER 10

The Making of a Servant of the Church

103

CHAPTER 11

The Psychological Health of the Servant

111

CHAPTER 12

The Spiritual Education of the Servant

127

Preface

We have in this short work Matthew the Poor's quintessential statement on the nature of Christian service. In order that we may understand the great abbot's message and glean the most benefit from this spiritual gem, a few words of explanation are in order. Firstly, the reader must bear in mind the wide and diffuse meaning the author ascribes to the word *servant*. In the Coptic Church, the word is a broad designation for anyone rendering any type of good deed within the confines of the Church. The person sitting on the episcopal chair and the person mopping the floors of the parish hall are both granted the title. Of course, the one is accorded a much higher rank and esteem than the other; but both contribute, in their relative degrees, to the common "service" of Christ's flock.

A servant, in the sense employed by Abba Matta, therefore, may or may not be ordained and does not necessarily fill a professional role. There is no demand for formal credentials; all that is needed is a willing heart. It is not strange to see a layman mount the pulpit of a Coptic church on a Sunday morning to deliver the homily. I have seen lay men, women, and young people formally address the congregation while clergy sit and listen. And I personally believe all this to be exactly in line with the felicitous words of the great Fr. Alexander Schmemann: "To be *priest* is from a profound point of view the most natural thing in the world. Man was created priest of the world, the one who offers the world to God in a sacrifice of love and praise and who, through this eternal eucharist, bestows the divine life upon the world."[1]

As a result, the title of "servant" is sometimes bestowed quite lavishly, one might almost say recklessly, upon any believer who volunteers even a tiny morsel of his or her time to aid in the functions of the Church. But this is not a criticism. It is a reflection of the laudable attempts made by the ordained clergy of the Coptic Church to convince the unordained laity that every single one of them is *called*—in one way or another—to take up Christ's challenge to His Apostles to be a part of the Church's mission to the world. St. Mark records the Lord's celebrated phrase "whoever desires to become great among you shall be your servant"; but to assume that Christ intended these words only for His disciples, and not for the rest of humanity, would be to miss the universal breadth of the Gospel. One must remember, therefore, that when Abba Matta speaks in this book about the "church servant," he is speaking generally about the person who wishes to invest time and energy into doing good for the sake of others. The reader will encounter sections in the book, on the other hand, in which the author speaks directly to ordained clergy; and in such passages the message will be crafted to fit their particular needs.

This is not a book one can breeze through; the author's thoughts often challenge us and sometimes unsettle us, but we need the exhortation. I am convinced that this work will unquestionably reward the focused and attentive reader. It has been remarked to me on several occasions that some paragraphs in Abba Matta's books must be read two or three times to be fully comprehended; indeed, I had to read certain paragraphs in the present work six to seven times in order to

---

1   Alexander Schmemann, *For the Life of the World* (Crestwood, NY: SVS Press, 2002), p. 92.

translate them adequately. The point is that the reader ought not to lose heart if he or she finds it necessary to go over the same passage multiple times. We are not reading a modern newspaper, but drawing on ancient Christian wisdom that hails back to the days of the Apostles. It is my sincere hope that every person who passes through these pages will sense a fresh impulse to gird the waist and shoe the feet for the spreading of God's gospel of peace.

Introduction

Necessity has driven us to offer this series of essays to draw the reader's attention to a very important fact: that there is an enormous difference between religious "knowledge," as it is marketed in modern days, and "service" according to its original Christian meaning. Religious instruction, even when offered in a spiritual manner, tends to focus on the cultivation of the mind, the interpretation of the Bible, the development of religious exercises such as hymnology and prayer, the refinement of preaching skills, and the accumulation of bits of knowledge in history, tradition, and theology. The end result of this process is often a self-admiring contentment and a feeling of superiority over others in spiritual matters.

Christian service, in contrast, focuses on the catechization and reproof of oneself, mastery of the bodily desires (to free the spirit from its bondage to personal whims and tendencies), and the adoption of a warm and constant state of repentance in order to receive God's grace. The end result of this process is usually self-abandonment, the surrender of oneself to God, the forging of an open and honest relationship with others, and a constant and reverent engagement in worship.

We may say, then, that while religious instruction (without service) tends to inflate its object—the Gospel says, "Knowledge puffs up but love edifies" (1 Cor. 8:1)—Christian service fills the spirit with reverence, love, and humility. For this reason, we consider it necessary to discuss the qualities that make up *spiritual* service, so that barren instruction and teaching do not become burdensome to the soul.

First, we need to understand the significant difference between a *religious teacher* and a *spiritual servant*. The first relays information; the second builds souls. The first extracts knowledge from books and places it before the student on paper. The second feeds the ones he serves from his own fullness: he shares the inner riches of his faith, his love, his self-sacrifice, and his humility. He provides genuine experiences and a living example to those he serves, for it is *himself* that he gives, and it is *his own life* that he offers. The first transmits words and concepts that he has heard externally. The second brings forth words and concepts from within, an outpouring that rises from his depths, like lava erupting from the depths of the earth. The first prepares a lesson to convince his listeners; the second labors to give birth to children in Christ.

Therefore, we must say that there is also a difference between the student who sits for instruction in religion with the promise that he will receive rewards and accolades for memorizing his lessons, and the obedient servant who places his hand into the hand of his spiritual guide and follows his counsel with reverence. Such a guide will be constantly asking himself the question, "What can this servant do to overcome his sin and grow in the spirit?" The first increases every day in knowledge, strives to outdo his rivals, and boasts of his achievements. The second increases in grace and humility daily and strives even more to go unnoticed and unapplauded by others (even himself).

To summarize, the Christian servant is not just a teacher of lessons, but is in the first place a leader of souls to salvation. The first priority and central preoccupation of Christian service is to lead the souls of men and women to repentance and to train the young in the paths of virtue and the fear of God.

✠ ✠ ✠

The lesson of love can never be taught simply by prearranged words and anecdotes. Rather, it is taught by truly giving yourself and communicating the love and longing for Christ to those you serve. The servant's spiritual children will feel a contact with God's love through the warmth of his love. They will taste the love that is handed down to them from God as an inheritance is handed down from father to son.

The lesson of truthfulness and integrity cannot be taught simply by sharing a few words, reciting a few Bible verses, or singing nice songs. It is delivered through the tough and thorny task of leading spiritual children one by one over the rocky and costly pathway of life, by encouraging them, protecting them, and supporting them. The servant helps them carry their burdens and shares their losses and humiliations.

The lesson of humility cannot be taught by intellectual persuasion, but only by a prolonged and bitter struggle against one's ego. It is a bitter and painful lesson to learn, something a human being can never endure alone without the aid of a helping hand to cover such dangerous ground. Sometimes the faithful hand of support must raise the soul from the stumbling block of low self-esteem, while at other times it will need to lower the soul into the dust—that is, to act as a sieve to filter out the impurities of self-conceit and pride.

The lesson of purity cannot be taught by informing spiritual children of lofty ideals, or by describing historical examples, or by training them in rules or techniques. Rather, it comes first and foremost through the servant's willingness to scrub out the spots in his children's lives. A mother cannot tolerate seeing her child covered in filth; therefore, she patiently and persistently cleans her child on a daily basis. The servant does the same thing to his child's spiritual filth, not with resentment, but rather with the hope of seeing his eventual reformation—a change achieved without inciting guilt, fear, or conflict. This learning process continues until the spiritual child outgrows all the weaknesses of childhood. If a shortcoming of the servant renders the child unable to shed any particular weakness, the servant perseveres until the child finally overcomes it in adulthood.

When real and true lessons such as these are taught to a spiritual child, eternal life will grow within him. He will confront his own questions, not the questions of others. These lessons will lift him up, not above others in knowledge, but above himself, by conquering his own whims and desires. They will give him the pleasure of being lowliest of all, of taking last place. They will prepare him not to write a book, but to recognize Christ's grace and to perceive his own flaws and sins.

The mind does not assimilate these lessons through memorization or accumulation of facts. Instead, the lessons are learned when a servant leads a soul through the fields of the spirit. Then the counsels and reproofs of the servant may be converted to faith, hope, and love in the children, and they may become manifest in their conduct and character. Such lessons are not relayed by paper, wood, or ink, but by the power of the Spirit in the heart and conscience, and through the revelation of Christ in the depths of the soul. They are further reinforced by the inspiration of the lives of the fathers, prophets, and saints of old, and by the stories in the Bible, daily recalled to memory. The examinations, rewards, and incentives of Christian service are not just about giving out little pictures or sweets; they are the successes and failures that the servant himself experiences and that the children undergo when struggling to obey the commands of Christ. The lesson is not given at an appointed hour but throughout the course of one's life. The "final exam" does not come at the end of the year, but on Judgment Day.

How awesome and dignified is Christian service! And how good is the trustworthy and loyal servant who can say along with Christ, "Learn from Me, for I am gentle and lowly in heart" (Matt. 11:29). "You call Me Teacher and Lord, and you say well, for *so* I am. If I then, *your* Lord and Teacher, have washed your feet, you also ought to wash one another's feet. For I have given you an example, that you should do as I have done to you" (John 13:13–15).

Matthew the Poor
The Monastery of St. Macarius
November 8, 1971
The Feast of St. Macarius, Bishop of Assiut

PART ONE

The Nature of Christian Service

CHAPTER I

Love: The Ultimate Criterion of Christian Service

*Though I bestow all my goods to feed the poor,
and though I give my body to be burned, but have not love,
it profits me nothing. (1 Cor. 13:3)*

Love is the ultimate criterion of Christ's service. Any criterion used to measure our service, other than love, is a merely human measurement. This criterion of love rests on three basic foundations:

1. *Love for God* as the driving motive of every service rendered, from the smallest to the greatest: "Simon, *son* of Jonah, do you love Me? . . . Tend My sheep" (John 21:15, 16)
2. *Love for those served* as the images of Christ: "Assuredly, I say to you, inasmuch as you did *it* to one of the least of these My brethren, you did *it* to Me" (Matt. 25:40)
3. *Love for the Church* as the body of Christ and dedication to protecting it from degeneration and weakness: "Even so you, since you are zealous for spiritual *gifts*, let it be for the edification of the church *that* you seek to excel" (1 Cor. 14:12).

The Distortion of Love

There are many factors that contribute to the distortion of Christian love—the desire for monetary gain or personal advancement, and so on. But the most dangerous factor is a certainty of one's personal godliness. When service becomes merely a showcase for one's own piety, self-righteousness begins to grow in the place of holy love. The reason this is the most damaging factor is as follows: while the falsehood of all the other factors is easily revealed with time (leading to their eventual disintegration), this particular factor deceives the servant to the last by making his service look vibrant and successful from the outside. The deception can be prolonged almost indefinitely, while the work remains a "service" lacking in any spiritual gifts or worthiness before God.

Three Distortions of Christian Love

1. Excessive concern with "results." The servant experiences joy in times of success but despair in times of failure.
2. Excessive attention paid to the administration and minute details of service more than to the souls being served. This results in the sacrifice of souls to maintain the order of the system.
3. A lack of growth of love among those served. An extension of this is an excessive attachment to the servant, rather than to God.

CHAPTER 2

Qualities of the Christian Servant

1. *The Call*

Since this service is the Lord's, the Lord Himself must call those who will serve Him. The Lord does not call someone unless He sees love for God, longing for God, and faithfulness to God in the heart of the servant. And since serving God is equivalent to serving His little children, it is vital that the person whom the Lord calls be inspired by feelings of compassion, mercy, and sympathy for the weak and downtrodden.

Therefore, a calling to serve is confirmed by the presence of a heart filled with love and faithfulness toward God on the one hand, and compassion and sympathy toward others on the other. When these signs are found, a person can be sure that he is called by God to serve Him.

The call of God is not accompanied by voices or dreams, but rather by the gift of the necessary spiritual qualities for Christian service. These spiritual gifts are usually small to begin with, but they grow with consistent practice and prayer.

2. The Spirit of Discipleship

No one is called to serve while in a state of perfection. Nor can there ever be a servant of the Lord, no matter how rich in spiritual gifts, who does not need to preserve the heart and mind of a disciple for the rest of his life. Moreover, such a servant must toil every day to discover his deficiencies and flaws. He must not be unsettled by the rebukes of the Holy Spirit that come from the mouths of others. Finally, he must never discount criticism or advice, wherever he may encounter it. Such an open spirit will allow the Lord's servant to increase constantly in love for God and man.

3. The Ability to Detect and Battle Inner Selfishness

The servant who is called by God is quick to perceive his own selfishness and to examine honestly how it lurks behind everything he says and does. He begins to recognize which personal inclinations are tainted by egotism, and he battles them by sober living, vigils, prayer, tears, and taking a firm stand against himself. No servant is completely free of egotism, but the most problematic servant is the one who does not at least perceive its presence within himself.

The truly successful servant does not fear the exposure of his faults. He does not shrink from recalling, and apologizing for, any sinful word or deed inspired by his egotism. The ministry of such of servant remains at a very high level. Such humility encourages personal growth as well as the growth of love among his spiritual children. In addition, the consistent practice of confession severs the bonds of egotism and selfishness, because the confession of sins always gives renewed strength to the soul.

4. Working for the Benefit of the Ones Being Served

Christian service is not concerned only with delivering a message, transmitting knowledge, or even doing deeds of mercy. Rather, it is essentially about forging a fatherly connection between the servant and the ones he serves: "My beloved and longed-for brethren, my joy and crown" (Phil. 4:1); and "My little children, for whom I labor in birth again until Christ is formed in you" (Gal. 4:19). The love that exists between the servant and the ones served depends on the servant sacrificing one essential thing: *himself.* He gives his faith, love, sincerity, and zeal for the sake of increasing their faith, love, sincerity, and zeal for God and for one another. Thus, in a way, Christian service resembles raising a child: "We were gentle among you, just as a nursing *mother* cherishes her own children" (1 Thess. 2:7). Service, then, is a spiritual motherhood (or a sacrificial fatherhood), where the servant sacrifices not only physical things but all things, as Christ Himself did.

A servant can neither benefit the ones he serves nor feed their souls with love, faith, and hope unless he first maintains a strong connection with God, by whom all such gifts are given. A successful servant does not receive these gifts from God primarily for the sake of serving others, but rather for his own salvation. Then, from his own abundance, he can give good things to others, while himself always remaining full: "Let your light so shine before men, that they may see your good works and glorify your Father in heaven" (Matt. 5:16). But the servant who feeds on God's gifts only for the sake of returning them to others usually remains empty and toils in vain.

Once the flame of love for Christ is kindled in the servant's heart, this is a sign of a great potential for spiritual gifts. It indicates the servant's readiness to receive spiritual things from God. This is why a continual bond with the Lord is both the door to spiritual gifts and the secret to effectively benefiting others, which is so necessary in this service.

5. Openness or Honesty

When the service is contaminated by self-seeking, skewing its spiritual balance, it becomes continually overcautious, cowardly, and predisposed to retreat. It will become a service unprepared for any sort of loss, constantly halting and regressing. The servant himself tends to measure "gains" versus "losses" by mere statistics.

Conversely, if it is a healthy service, as attested by a profound love in the heart, you will find the servant bold, candid, with a ready tongue. He is prepared to bear any burden, because the true love that comes from God compels him to forget himself and convert every loss into a gain. One of the unique and unmistakable signs of such love is a pleasure in self-sacrifice and a commitment to self-abandonment.

There is also a false type of openness and honesty whose basis is not love but rather egotism. It thrives on the love of show, the exhibition of one's merits, and proving oneself. Such openness only stirs up trouble, conflict, and defiance. Every servant must beware this defect because it only harms the service of Christ.

In contrast, true candor in service is meek and yielding—like love itself, always smiling—and never causes harm or disgrace to anyone. It might at times need to express itself with fiery words; but it is nevertheless driven by a humble heart, a kind face, and tearful eyes: "We cannot but speak the things we have seen and heard" (Acts 4:20). True openness glorifies Christ and prolongs the service for many years.

6. Impartiality

A principal cause of failure in our Christian service, which leads to the dispersion of our sheep and to the rise of such vices as malice, envy, and anger, is showing favoritism or partiality toward a particular soul or group of souls. Christ favored the weak, the outcast, and the marginalized, for they needed a courageous love. But with courageous love comes great responsibility. He who favors the sinner and the outcast actually shares their burden of sin and takes a "holy portion" of their dishonor: "When they saw *it*, they all complained, saying, 'He has gone to be a guest with a man who is a sinner'" (Luke 19:7).

In Christian service, we cannot sacrifice the weak and diseased sheep for the sake of preserving our relationship with the healthy flock. Christ left the ninety-nine healthy sheep to search for the one that had gone astray. It is a troubling thing when love inclines itself toward a particular person because of his strength, beauty, or charm, because this means that the servant himself is sick and in need of treatment.

There is also a type of "love" in service that is merely interested in pleasing superiors or in gaining the favor of those in authority more than in following the truth, keeping the commandments, or honoring Christ. The danger in this sort of "love" is that it degrades a service that is essentially worship to God: "For if I still pleased men, I would not be a bondservant of Christ" (Gal 1:10). It is vital that the Christian servant be steered by the Holy Spirit, not the opinions of men: "For as many as are led by the Spirit of God, these are sons of God" (Rom. 8:14).

7. Spiritual Simplicity

When a servant draws his knowledge solely from books, it is hard for him to have spiritual simplicity. Books swell knowledge, and "knowledge puffs up" (1 Cor. 8:1). Moreover, when one excels in knowledge and in verbal exposition, where the excellence is not spiritual but merely intellectual, the servant may be deluded into thinking he may use these gifts to demonstrate his personal skills. This may further lead to a dangerous kind of attachment on the part of his spiritual children, an enthusiastic preference for his teaching alone, and an unhealthy desire to be just like him: "And I, brethren, when I came to you, did not come with excellence of speech or of wisdom declaring to you the testimony of God. . . . And my speech and my preaching *were* not with persuasive words of human wisdom, but in demonstration of the Spirit and of power, that your faith should not be in the wisdom of men but in the power of God" (1 Cor. 2:1, 4, 5).

He who has spiritual simplicity is naturally drawn to the simplicity of the Kingdom of God. He speaks only what he receives; and he calls others to that true simplicity that was repeatedly exhorted by Christ when He taught us to return to the childlike simplicity that is the only pathway to the Kingdom of God.

When a person serves others through excellent speech, relying on human means of knowledge more than on the inspiration of the Holy Spirit, he cheats the sheep, leads them away from the way of the Kingdom, and undermines his own calling. This is because the sheep will cling to him and trust in his knowledge; therefore, the servant effectively crucifies the truth of Christ. For these reasons, it is imperative that the servant rely on the simplicity of the Holy Spirit and strive to avoid places of honor. The servant must take a step back so that the Holy Spirit may step forward. He must conceal himself so that Christ alone may be revealed.

The servant must be always vigilant to weigh the words and opinions that inform his teaching against the dictates of the Holy Spirit and the requirements of love. This will prevent him from falling into the errors of human wisdom and human opinion: "I will not dare to speak of any of those things which Christ has not accomplished through me" (Rom. 15:18).

8. Spiritual Fellowship with Those One Serves

The spiritual fellowship between the servant and his children can profoundly influence their feelings and thoughts. Therefore, this fellowship is an integral part of Christian service. Before anything else, service is a *stooping* to the natural level of the children to understand their actual state in life. Such stooping also helps the servant find out the extent of their ignorance, spiritual poverty, darkness, and estrangement from God. It is, thereafter, an actual *lifting-up* of the children to a higher state, by virtue of the Holy Spirit's action, by the light of the commandments, and by the power of faith, hope, and love.

Christian service can never be "above" even the filthiest states to which a human soul may degenerate, and it must never scorn a soul for its foulness. Service is not words preached from a pulpit, but rather the act of grasping the hands of a weak and sinful soul and leading it from darkness to light, from death to life.

Emotional fellowship with someone suffering from a bodily illness or injury is a beautiful thing. But spiritual fellowship with someone living in sin—something that involves the scorn and rejection of others—is incomparably more beautiful. It is, in fact, the very work for which Christ was incarnate: "He made Him who knew no sin *to be* sin for us, that we might become the righteousness of God in Him" (2 Cor. 5:21). A servant can never succeed in raising a soul from the pits of despair, darkness, and death unless he is prepared by faith and love to enter with that soul into the same pits. He must also be armed with the hope that he will be raised to new life and light by the power of God: "Not an elder or an angel, but the Lord Himself saved them from all their tribulation, because He loved them and spared them" (Is. 63:9 OSB).

9. Constant Awareness of One's Weakness

A servant will not be able to sympathize with the weak and outcast if he does not first live with the constant awareness of his own weakness, his own inadequacy. For the moment a servant begins to feel certain of himself, and the conviction of his personal superiority and power grows within him, a dangerous rift forms between him and those he serves. The children begin to feel the formation of a deep gulf separating them from the lofty heights of their servant. The result is either despair at the impossibility of ever reaching his eminence or the inclination to deify him and surround his head with a halo of sanctity. In either case, God is not glorified, of whom it was said, "He was crucified in weakness" (2 Cor. 13:4).

It is good for a servant always to remember his sins and not to forget them with the excuse that they have been forgiven. He will then refuse to scoff at the sins of the children he serves, regardless of their number or severity, because the good servant does not rely on anything except grace. And he always puts himself in the place of the weak, lest he be found unworthy before God. The good servant must furthermore appear to his children as a weak human being in need of God's help and grace, for it is only through weakness that God reveals His power: "My grace is sufficient for you, for My strength is made perfect in weakness" (2 Cor. 12:9).

When the children clearly perceive the natural and weak state of their servant, they will ascribe all the success of the service, all the power of the preaching, and all other achievements directly to God Himself. And thus, all the honor of the service will go to its only true source: "We have this treasure in earthen vessels, that the excellence of the power may be of God and not of us" (2 Cor. 4:7).

10. Acceptance of All Servants in the Church Without Distinction

Even if he has apostolic strength, no servant is capable of gathering up and serving all of God's flock in the world. Christ alone is capable of such a feat. He has shared His powers with His servants so that together they might accomplish the work of Christ. If a servant ignores his fellow servants, raises himself above them, or in any way deprecates them, he injures Christ's work. He unwittingly infects the sheep with the spirit of division, conflict, and favoritism. Any service that splinters into partisan groups is not from God and can only harm the Church. But a servant who is called by God to do His work always gathers together with Christ and does not scatter. He teaches the sheep how to love every servant in the Church, as well as one another, in Christ's name.

The only way to spare the sheep from any stumbling blocks to be found in others' service is to teach them what is right and to persuade them of the truth. If we criticize other servants in front of them, we only teach them how to be judgmental and quarrelsome, thereby estranging them from the simplicity of life in Christ and the Kingdom. Any servant who is tempted to criticize or judge his fellow servant should remember that every person has his own particular talents, and it is never right for the strong to ridicule the weak, nor for the weak to ridicule the strong.

When a servant's love for his fellow servants is demonstrated to the children in a clear and genuine light, it serves as the cornerstone for the spread of the spirit of unity and harmony within the Church. If unity was Christ's ultimate aim in His work of redemption—that all believers would become one in Him and in the Father—and if love is the divine means of effecting that sacred unity in God, then clearly the servant's first task is to instruct his children in divine love by providing them with a living example of it: "By this all will know that you are My disciples, if you have love for one another" (John 13:35).

CHAPTER 3

The Essence of Christian Service

The appearance of service is one thing. The essence of service is something entirely different.

The appearance of service involves outward forms: sermons, rites, particular activities organized to serve the needs of the children, the division of responsibilities among the servants in charge, teaching servants through the prior experience of older servants and from books, and providing new servants with the necessary tools of service.

The essence of service, on the other hand, is the transmission of eternal life to the children whom God has placed in our charge: "From that time Jesus began to preach and to say, 'Repent, for the kingdom of heaven is at hand'" (Matt. 4:17). And the transmission of eternal life involves a person's acceptance of the work Christ accomplished for his sake, which He also bequeathed to the Church for its transmission to any and every person who believes in it through the Gospel and the Holy Mysteries.

In fact, it is not difficult to accomplish the external aspect of Christian service. It may be done by anyone. However, no human being, no matter how virtuous or talented, can accomplish the essence of Christian service on his own. Service touches God's own life; therefore, it cannot be successfully accomplished by ordinary, visible means. The essence of service is a deeply mystical thing, far beyond human nature. Only if we correctly understand the inner essence of service can we avoid repeating any past mistaken attempts to accomplish it.

1. *Living Faith*

On the one hand, the simplest picture one can form of the power of living faith is its ability to move mountains and trees from one place to another, as the Lord Jesus said (Mark 11:23; Luke 17:6). Furthermore, the Lord said this feat was possible within the narrowest limits of faith—even if faith is the size of a mustard seed. Despite the small size of the mustard seed, it carries within it the *potential for life*. What moves trees and mountains is not an indolent faith, as it were, but a living faith. Therefore, what is needed for active faith is a pulsating life, not the natural life that is latent in the mustard seed, but eternal life, the life of God. Or, to put it another way, man must believe in God and live by Him.

On the other hand, the greatest picture one can form of the power of faith is the ability to transmit the experience of eternal life into the hearts of others by love and admonition, to the point that they receive it and live it out in the Church: "The life was manifested, and we have seen, and bear witness, and declare to you that eternal life which was with the Father and was manifested to us—that which we have seen and heard we declare to you, that you also may have fellowship with us" (1 John 1:2, 3).

This is the essence of Christian service—to tell others about the eternal life by which we live, with the hope that they might eventually experience it with us. The former and simpler picture of the power of faith—being able to move trees and mountains—is not absolutely expected or demanded of us. It is a power granted by God only in exceptional cases of pressing need. The latter and greater picture of faith—the transmission of the experience of eternal life from heart to heart—is a necessity placed upon every believer who is given that life: "Let him who hears say, 'Come!'" (Rev. 22:17). This living faith that comprises such a vital part of the essence of service is given freely and generally to everyone who accepts it.

A living faith is a faith that fully believes that God is able to raise the dead. For that reason, it never considers the repentance of a sinner an overly difficult thing, even if the sin be worthy of death. Consequently, those who possessed a living faith cannot bear the sight of unrepentant sinners; neither do they ever flag in their service, even if threatened with death.

Living faith subsists on a full trust in God and never ceases to rely on His primary title and attribute—"Almighty." Faith never abandons the conviction that He will fulfill all that He has promised. Thus, the fruits of living faith depend on this conviction and trust in God's word. If living faith (and the conviction and trust that accompany it) were ever removed from the service, then all that would remain would be the appearance of service.

2. The Mystery of Christ

If a person is a true Christian believer, in the sense that he lives by the Spirit of Christ and obeys His commands, he has entered into the mystery of the new creation—a thing no man can explain or describe, regardless of his knowledge. Christ Himself said that this mystery is worked out by the Holy Spirit beyond the knowledge of man, just like a gust of wind that blows wherever it wills (John 3:8).

The essence of service involves the servant's formation of a spiritual child into a true Christian. In other words, the servant must achieve the incomprehensible and inexpressible mystery of Christ in his spiritual child. Again, the essence of service is not just about teaching and exposition of doctrines; it is about bequeathing the mystery of Christ (which transcends the mind) to the ones served. And the mystery of Christ is not transmitted by special knowledge or even virtuous conduct, but rather by receiving Christ's life and Spirit. He who has the Spirit of Christ has Christ Himself, and he who lacks the Spirit of Christ does not belong to Christ: "If anyone does not have the Spirit of Christ, he is not His" (Rom. 8:9).

To put it another way, the essence of service is not mere tutelage in rules and ideas, but the delivery of a certain spirit and life: "No one can say that Jesus is Lord except by the Holy Spirit" (1 Cor. 12:3).

Once the Christian servant realizes what the essence of service really is, he will immediately look inside himself (rather than into a book) to see if that essence is present in his heart. Books and manuals represent the external aspect of service and can play an important role, but without the spirit and life of Christ, what good are the best books and lessons? And when we turn to the Church, how it once was and still is, we find that she relays the mystery of Christ to believers in ways small and large. That is, she relays it by preaching and teaching, but ultimately what is preached and taught from the pulpit must be communicated practically and mystically through the seven sacraments.

Therefore, the basis of service is not to be found simply in formal teaching, for teaching constitutes merely the external aspect. The essential and mystical aspect cannot be imparted with words, but only by conveying the life and spirit of Christ to the children's hearts. If the Church relies solely on preaching and dispenses with its mysteries, it loses the mystical essence of service. From that point, it can hardly be called the Church.

The same applies to the individual service of each servant. If a servant comes to rely solely on the service of the tongue, without relying on the inward Spirit, he becomes a symbol of a Church devoid of mysteries. Any servant can display the outward appearance of service, but it is impossible for any servant to transmit spirit and life to his children unless he first carries the Spirit and Life of Christ.

3. *The Mystery of Love*

"Love" is one thing, and the "mystery of love" is something else. A human being may experience love (even pure love) and remain unchanged. But when a human being experiences the mystery of love, he does not remain the same. At that very moment, he learns self-sacrifice.

Christian love is not limited to itself. All other types of human love are concerned with the self and incline to death and decay, whereas Christian love is ever-living, and it breaks out and expands in every direction. It is a love that can grow and thrive even in the worst of circumstances. Christian love is stronger than death itself, for it contains within it the mystery of Christ's Resurrection and eternal life.

Therefore, there can be no sincere and active service without the presence of this mystical love, for active service needs the power to resurrect weak and dying souls. This will never happen without the power of love. Any servant can relay the words and teachings of Christ to others without losing a thing—he might even earn fame and accolades—but the servant who strives to relay the true essence of service (spirit and life) to others is in absolute need of the mystery of Christian love.

And it is clear from the words of the Apostle Paul (1 Cor. 13) that no matter how zealous or diligent a given service may be, if Christian love is lacking, it will ultimately profit nothing. A given service can be full of zeal and power even when driven by personal motives, but without true love, it is a service that is human, dead, and ineffective.

It proves to benefit neither the servant, nor the served, nor Christ. The mystery of Christian love raises the service from the human level to Christ's level. Christian love does not necessarily prompt a person to sacrifice his body, since it is after all possible to give one's body to be burned not in order to display Christ's love, but to display mere human courage or even to spite someone.

It can also be said that Christian love is like the magnetic needle of a compass. It could potentially point in any direction, but it happens to feel a strong pull toward magnetic north. The north magnetic pole has complete control over its movements. In the same way, Christ has complete control over the movements, the actions, the motives, and the zeal of the servant, by virtue of that mystical love that binds the servant to Christ forever.

Thus, if the service is inspired by the love of Christ and the power that pulls the servant toward Him, the smallest effort and sacrifice will have a positive effect on the children served, in the sense that the children's hearts will also feel the pull toward Christ and will be filled with His love. The servant who is moved by the mystery of love has the ability to pull others to Christ's love, and that is the essence of Christian service. If the service ever loses touch with the mystery of Christ's love, it will turn into a form of mere bodily exercise, a display of personal talent, or even simply a career choice. Love protects the service from self-righteousness and preserves the true faith.

No matter how much the rich young man excelled in religious instruction and kept the law, he lacked the necessary love to carry out the ultimate sacrifice of his possessions and to follow Christ (see Mark 10:17–31). Good and true instruction will bring us closer to the Kingdom of God; however, we will not enter it without that complete sacrifice and perfect self-surrender that love alone can achieve.

4. The Power of Prayer

The power of prayer forms a mystical link between the servant and the ones served, since it creates a union of their hearts and minds. Prayer prepares and energizes the servant; without the power of prayer, even the best of the servant's abilities remain confined within himself.

Prayer that is fervent and earnest erases the servant's "presence" from his mind and dissolves his selfishness, which then prepares the servant to give of himself without arrogance. The Spirit of God rests easily on this kind of person, and He will speak to the souls of the children through the servant's heart and tongue without any hindrance.

Prayer opens the hearts of the children to enlighten their eyes and heal their souls. It transforms them into pure, clear vessels for the reception of the Holy Spirit. The Spirit may then descend into their hearts free of the obstacles of argument, disputation, and doubt.

Prayer causes the Holy Spirit to intervene and remove the barriers that separate the servant from his children, particularly the barriers erected by the social environment, incorrect teaching, and snares laid by the enemy to thwart the communication of truth.

The power of prayer transforms calm words into thunder and lightning that rouse sleepy consciences from the stupor of sin; it softens stony hearts and calms a mind bent on conflict.

Prayer waters the dryness that afflicts the heart; it repels the spirit of opposition; it breaks the traps of the enemy; and it causes the adversaries of the service to flee. The will of God is revealed in prayer, and by prayer God casts out His net to catch good souls that will glorify Him, proclaim His name, do His will, and witness to His righteousness.

By prayer talents are given, gifts are dispersed, faith grows, and souls that were chained by sin are liberated. The once-enslaved people march out laden with the spoils of the Holy Spirit.[2] Prayer can be thought of as a horse's bit. When it is properly secured in our mouths, it enables God to steer the service wherever He wills.

Prayer is an adornment of grace for the servant. When his children see the reflection of their heavenly Bridegroom in his face, they are seized by a holy jealousy to possess Him too.

Prayer stamps the seal of the Holy Spirit's splendor on the faces of the children, diffuses among them the fragrance of heaven, and leads them all to God's good pleasure.

By prayer, all the glory and honor of service are attributed to God. To Him people will ascribe all blessing, majesty, wisdom, and authority, giving thanks to God, who has privileged us with the calling of servants.

2 An allusion to the exodus of the Israelites from their former enslavement, bearing the spoils of Egypt.

CHAPTER 4

Those We Serve

As long as there is a Good Shepherd, there will be a good flock. However, the sheep of the flock will have a variety of capabilities. There will also be examples of weaker members, such as those sheep that are sick, still suckling, or young. The Good Shepherd guides such a flock with wisdom and never resents its weaker members.

Many among us consider themselves to be "shepherds," although we are all in reality nothing more than weak sheep. And many of us, despite our outward appearance of piety and sanctity, are sick in God's sight, "dead in trespasses and sins" (Eph. 2:1), even lost far away from the flock. Our central ailment is that we are ignorant of our state. Despite the presence of sin in our lives, we remain complacent and turn a blind eye to our problem. That is, we are like a sheep whose organs have been infected after eating poisoned grass, and despite symptoms of discomfort, it goes on eating the grass because of its pleasant taste. The sheep stands among the rest of the sheep looking as if everything is fine while the poison courses through its body. In the same way, many of us sit in church looking virtuous while ingesting sin.

A necessary condition for the fruition of the service in the lives of the ones we serve is their purification from within. That is, their hearts must be purified for the reception of God's Spirit and His gifts. Otherwise, the service will not bear fruit in their lives; they will be like a sheep whose digestive organs are so stricken with disease that it cannot benefit from even the finest pastures.

CHAPTER 5

Diseases of the Flock

1. Complaints about Entering the Narrow Gate

This is the plague of the modern age. Everybody wants to relax and enjoy life, and the world has specialized in providing us with all sorts of different ways to lead an easy life. The world has learned how to harness people's minds and money in order to sell them relaxation at the cheapest price possible. The Kingdom of God, however, requires a person to inconvenience himself, to refuse ease, and to resist pleasure. Which of these two alternatives are people likely to choose?

Either a person will side with the world and its pleasures (and so enter by the wide gate), thereby realizing his personal pleasures and losing himself in endless entertainment and enjoyments, or he will side with God and His love (and so enter the narrow gate), thereby realizing holiness and toil. Such a person will find joy in life with God.

It is impossible for a person to combine the delights of the body with the delights of the Spirit. It is impossible for a person to find agreement between the gratification of the body and the consolations of grace. Accursed is the shepherd who teaches his flock to drink from the well of sin, and accursed is the flock that eats such poison and calls other sheep to join them. If you are a shepherd who desires to rejoice in having a plentitude of sheep, and if you pride yourself on the immense size of your audience, then beware the widening of the narrow gate! The Lord's gate will forever remain narrow, and those who consent to pass through it will forever remain few. The servants of the present generation who try to stretch the gate to fit the weaknesses of the children they serve, whether to suit their tastes or to satisfy their requests, do not lead them to eternal life but rather to destruction.

This is our duty: "Denying ungodliness and worldly lusts, we should live soberly, righteously, and godly in the present age" (Titus 2:12).

2. Avoiding the Sword of the Word

"For the word of God *is* living and powerful, and sharper than any two-edged sword, piercing even to the division of soul and spirit, and of joints and marrow, and is a discerner of the thoughts and intents of the heart" (Heb. 4:12). We often turn a blind eye to certain verses in the Bible as we read them. When we run into certain commands, we do not stop to give them any thought. We are adept at avoiding the sermons and teachings that contain words directed at us, and we usually try to escape our conscience.

It is true that the Word is a double-edged sword, but who is holding the sword? It is God's own Word, for which He sacrificed Himself on the Cross to give us eternal life from the midst of darkness and death. If the sword is in the calm and meek hand of the Holy Spirit, it will be thrust into man to divide the old self that seeks the world from the eternal spirit that seeks life.

Why do we despise these wounds of the Spirit? How do the spiritually sick expect to continue living without surrendering to the wounds caused by the thrust of that blade, down to the tissues of the heart? If only the children we serve could know the inestimable worth of that painful Word and of that piercing commandment whose aim is the healing of the deceitful heart, the degenerate conscience, the withered soul, and the diseased members. If they only knew that this sword can grant them purity of life, clarity of conscience, and the light of life, they would grasp it with their own hands and drive it into themselves to the depth of their hearts, to let out the black and fetid blood. They would endure every pain, every humiliation, and every affliction until the old man within them was finally dead.

If a person hears the Word of God but remains unwilling to allow it to penetrate his heart and expose the secrets of his conscience, or unwilling to fall under its blade to divide death from life, then the Word of salvation will become the Word of judgment.

Indeed, now is the time the Apostle Paul foretold to his disciple Timothy, when ears will be closed to the voice of truth, and people will turn to easy preaching and believe idle fables because their consciences are deprived of true and sincere rebukes: "For the time will come when they will not endure sound doctrine, but according to their own desires, *because* they have itching ears, they will heap up for themselves teachers; and they will turn *their* ears away from the truth, and be turned aside to fables" (2 Tim. 4:3, 4).

3. *Spiritual Old Age (or Senility)*

Just as a flock of sheep can suffer from the sterility of age, or as the symptoms of old age can begin to encroach upon a person in his younger years—the decline of health, the diminishing of the senses, and the hunching of the back—so also these symptoms may appear in Christian service, even at the height of its vitality and growth (in terms of the flock's life with God and progress toward holiness).

One cause of this phenomenon may be the dryness of the flock's pasture—that is, vacillating teaching or a lifeless example. Another cause may be the inordinate pursuit of bodily pleasures, something that drains the sap of life and spoils the fine taste of holiness. Another major cause is the excessive pursuit of money, material goods, or the tremendous number of other attractions in this world. Another cause may be the devotion of all one's time and health to the attainment of worldly position. Such position is usually not attained except by those who have given up most of their youth, vigor, and health (though they eventually come to regard all this work and exertion as an odious burden).

This spiritual senility means that people's ears are tired of hearing the constant calls for repentance and change of heart. In such cases, the preacher cries out to the listeners as though they were dead and motionless bodies, while each person looks at his neighbor as though his neighbor were the intended target and not he himself. Spiritual senility also means that people's eyes are tired of reading the Bible and spiritual books. The words stand on the page cold and lifeless, and the reader's eyes are scarcely able to pay attention and resist the approach of sleep. Spiritual senility means the heart has become stonelike, losing the ability to become inflamed by the Spirit, losing the ability to feel and respond to the work of grace. Such a person stands in church for prayer and can do nothing but yawn, yawn, yawn, to the point that he becomes a laughingstock to those around him. Meanwhile, he feels and understands nothing of what's happening, as though he were not even there.

Spiritual senility prevents true spiritual nourishment from bearing any real fruit. To the senile in spirit, the sacraments are dead rites, church services are just a cold set of routines, sermons are letdowns, and religious books are no better than some form of recreation. The Spirit within is quenched, and nothing remains in the heart except the whispers and bits of grace left over from the past life, which is all the person has left to resolve future problems.

This spiritual senility steals from a person the ability to make a determined and heartfelt return to God. No matter what lukewarm promises he makes to God that he will repent, he finds himself slinking little by little back to his former self. Every fresh attempt to repent only reveals his continuing descent into this senile and decrepit spiritual state. Unfortunately, there is no possibility of defeating spiritual senility except by crucifying the self, cutting off all nourishment for the old man, and emptying the self of all cares except the salvation of the soul. "But those who wait on God shall renew *their* strength; they shall mount up with wings like eagles" (Is. 40:31).

4. Idle Waste of Life

This is the subject of one of the petitions prayed by the priest in the absolution of the Midnight Hour:[3] that God protect His people from idly wasting this life, one of Satan's most frequent traps. If Satan succeeds in infecting a person with this psychological disease, he effectively disrupts the Holy Spirit's attempts to rouse the person from a lethargic state of apathy, thereby frustrating the servant's attempts to rouse the person to a state of zeal, worship, and holiness. In this state, the person may feel an inner stir from the counsels of his servants and through God's calling, but he lacks the motivation to obey those sacred voices. He feels that the zeal in his heart has dissipated because of his procrastination. Eventually, the voices completely cease to move him.

In our days, where can we find the zeal of the Apostle Paul: "I did not immediately confer with flesh and blood . . . but I went" (Gal. 1:16, 17)? Where is the immediate responsiveness of the Apostle Matthew when he heard Christ's voice while sitting in the tax-collector's

---

3 The popular Coptic prayer book, known as the *agpeya*, contains seven canonical "hours" which are to be prayed by the faithful every day and also includes an "absolution" that is meant to be prayed by the priest.

booth: "'Follow Me.' So he arose and followed Him" (Matt. 9:9)? Where is the fervor of the astonished crowd gathered on the day of Pentecost, who heard the discourse of the Apostle Peter and said, "Men *and* brethren, what shall we do" (Acts 2:37)?

When the people we serve become afflicted by this delirium and desire to delay everything spiritual, the years of teaching we have invested in them are rendered futile. They become senile and decrepit in soul, yet are still in need of baby food or even milk. The Apostle Paul says this to such people: "You have become dull of hearing. For though by this time you ought to be teachers, you need *someone* to teach you again the first principles of the oracles of God; and you have come to need milk and not solid food" (Heb. 5:11, 12).

The voice of truth does not strike a person's heart multiple times with equal force. If we refuse the voice of truth once, its rebuke and summons will be less clear and less powerful the second time, and this trend will continue until we start to doubt if it be God's voice at all. How sad this is! A person will never doubt God's voice as long as he diligently listens to it and obeys it from the start. Instead, we refuse to listen to the voice of truth because of our needless procrastination, delay, and waste of time in pursuit of our desires and sins. What follows is the loss of the inner spiritual antenna that detects God's voice. Finally, the time comes when we seek repentance diligently, with tears, but fail to find it: "He found no place for repentance, though he sought it diligently with tears" (Heb. 12:17).

5. Self-pity and Self-indulgence

If a vinedresser does not prune the vine, its branches will stagnate, and its fruit will rot. If a father fails to chastise his son out of pity, he will produce an insignificant man who is unable to bear real responsibilities. Similarly, if a servant leans toward indulgence of his children, desiring to earn their friendship, he corrupts the flock and destroys their potential to rise to the loftiest heights of Christian virtue, living faith, and sacrificial love.

When the flock suffers from this over-indulgence of the self; when they are deprived of the reproofs of the Word, resulting in the enfeebling of the servant and the loss of the Spirit; when they become resigned to the nemesis of laziness and deprecate the rebukes needed for their sins—then, not only does their growth come to a sudden stop, but they may also begin to question their servant and turn away from the path. Here the enemy seizes the opportunity to attack by planting the seeds of grumbling in their hearts. He tries to persuade them of the tremendous difficulties of the way and to incite fear of the dangers and trials that await. He then eases their entrance onto the broad and easy way, to facilitate their apostasy. How miserable is the man driven by self-pity, who has made self-indulgence the basis of his faith and behavior! The soul that is afflicted by self-pity will be driven straight to a life of ease, and from ease to a life of laziness, and from laziness to pleasure, from pleasure to sin, and from sin to death.

The way of God, in contrast, requires the strength of inward self-control, the will to rein in the self, the courage to face hardship, the patience to bear rebukes, and the ability to cheerfully accept reprimands when we err.

The Lord tells us to bear our cross, but what is a cross? The Lord has told us that the way is difficult, especially for the self-indulgent. Do we wish to be crowned without a struggle? And do we wish to carry on the struggle without being inwardly and outwardly tested? Do we suppose we will be able to stand before God on Judgment Day and apologize for our failure in the struggle by explaining that the commandments were just too hard to follow and the advice of our fathers and teachers was too hard to bear? Were not the commandments equally difficult for the fathers and teachers themselves?

"Convince, rebuke, exhort, with all longsuffering and teaching" (2 Tim. 4:2).

For truly—"Narrow *is* the gate and difficult *is* the way which leads to life, and there are few who find it" (Matt. 7:14).

CHAPTER 6

The Edification of the Christian Servant

1. Two Callings & Two Types of Edification

There are two basic callings in the church: one is monasticism, and the other is priesthood and church service. These two callings constitute a unified witness to Christ, and they both reflect direct obedience to the Lord's command. However, each entails a different system of life, a different pattern of behaviors, prayers, and duties.

He who is called to be a monk must build his entire mind and life on the examples of the desert fathers and always place before his eyes their first and greatest principle of *separation from the world and its positions of authority.* He must avoid becoming engaged in ministry to people in the world, no matter how much people beg him. It is mandatory that a monk cling with the greatest tenacity to this rule; otherwise, he may find himself in the end a monk bereft of monasticism, living by its name but without carrying its burden, speaking as its representative while being a stranger to its calling.

He who is called to be a priest or servant, to serve among people in the world, must build his entire mind and life on the examples of the apostolic fathers and always remember *their life of constant toil*

IF YOU LOVE ME

in ministering to the faithful, by day and by night, when convenient and when tiresome. It is mandatory that the servant cut off his own will and completely forgo all personal entitlement, personal wishes, and all dreams that tend to accompany such service (no matter how virtuous they may be in themselves). An example of a dream the servant must forgo is the urge to adopt a solitary life, to avoid people, and to be reluctant to speak to them—*except* in those instances where such behavior will increase the strength and success of the service itself. In other words, when such activities are performed not to please the self, but to heal its defects, they make a servant more effective for service.

One point that must be made clear to persons called to either of these vocations is this: *just as the monk is tempted by the lure of public service, so are the priest and servant tempted by the lure of the solitary life.* Both temptations are the complaints of an emotional desire to escape from one's reality. Sometimes this occurs as a result of past failures, but the truth is that a person need not be shaken by them. What he ought to do is to be strengthened in the Lord, stand before God, renew his personal covenant with Him, and be encouraged by the exemplary lives of the saints who have gone before him. By doing this, he will be able to reclaim his calling with zeal and diligence, finding in it his rest, his peace, and his crown.

The type of reading and study one pursues will have a dramatic impact on one's attitude toward his calling. Either it will increase his loyalty to his calling and further motivate him to fulfill its duties, or it will enfeeble his calling and cause its value to diminish in his eyes, until he slowly begins to develop a contempt for his work. Thus, when a monk neglects his reading from the lives and sayings of the desert fathers and focuses exclusively on Bible study, his spirit starts to recoil from the monastic vocation and solitary life. From there, he begins to entertain dreams of serving the public as a preacher

·⊹· 48 ·⊹·

and savior of souls. Little by little, a disdain for seclusion and for his monastery steals into his heart. Little by little, he comes to invent excuses for going back into the world or comes to imagine the presence of certain illnesses in his body or subconscious fears in his mind that demand his quick return to the world, throwing his vocation aside in the process.

Alternatively, if the priest or servant who has consecrated his life to the ministry of the Gospel neglects God's Word and fails to devote considerable time on a daily basis to sitting before it with open heart and mind to receive its guidance and counsel—instead becoming preoccupied with the stories of famous hermits, enamored by their miracles and solitude—he will shirk the toil and trials of his own service. He will begin to long for the eremitic life, to envy the monk's calling and way of life, and to imbibe desert wisdom. Little by little, waves of despair begin to roll over him and his service. He starts to doubt his calling, as though it were not suitable for him, or as though God were unjust in placing such a burden on a person who was naturally fitted to be a monk (as his faulty emotions tell him). His tongue becomes loosened and produces audible grumblings concerning his state, and his legs fly to the nearest monasteries, thus intensifying his confusion and widening the division in his soul. Every time he returns from a trip to the monasteries, he increasingly views his service as a trap he has fallen into or as a harsh prison. The reason this happens is that he started to build an imaginary tower of his own virtue and godliness. In the process, he turns his back on his poor church.

This does not mean the monk shouldn't immerse himself profoundly and persistently in the daily study of God's Word. Nor does it mean that the priest or servant shouldn't sit at the feet of the fathers and learn from their sayings, their chastity, and their asceticism. It means, rather, that the monk should allow the light of the Gospel to illumine his monastic, ascetic way. The priest in the world should allow the witness of the monastic path to motivate him in preaching the Word and to encourage him and those he serves in their witness *in* the world and *against* the world.

2. *Two Crucial Viewpoints in Service*

* The servant's view of God as the one who propels him forward in service with power.
* The servant's view of his own weaknesses, of which he is conscious every day.

These two viewpoints may initially seem to contradict each other, but in reality they form a perfect harmony. And we say this harmony is perfect because it is a union between God's power and man's weakness; therefore, it represents a harmony that is both natural and divine. God calls us to such discipleship: "My strength is made perfect in weakness" (2 Cor. 12:9). What is perfected here is God's power, not man's weakness, which, indeed, always remains weak.

Of course, if the priest or servant pays excessive attention to his own weakness and fails to remember the power of God (by which he serves and by whose authority he is directed), the harmony of viewpoints is destroyed, and he immediately falls. This is often a consequence of the servant's low self-esteem, which, in turn, is a result of his faith not yet being transfigured in his heart by the work of the sacred Blood. Hope has not yet been implanted into his soul by the eternal truth of the Resurrection. Likewise, if the priest or servant focuses exclusively on God's power and forgets his own weakness and sin, he will become inflated with arrogance and make himself into a god. He will remain ignorant of his true state until some sudden downfall or public calamity reveals his actual weakness.

We need to take a moment to further clarify the sharp difference between two kinds of self-awareness. On the one hand, there is the servant's acknowledgment of his true weakness, a sincerely humble attitude that neither diminishes his self-esteem nor damages his faith, instead strengthening the service and giving glory and honor to Christ. On the other hand, there is a gloomy admission of his weakness, a diseased form of "humility" that is fueled by despondency and low self-esteem.[4] This attitude destroys the work of faith and sabotages the service, and its ruinous effects become obvious when the shepherd shirks his duties and loses all courage. The difference between these two kinds of self-awareness is tremendous. The correct acknowledgment of our weakness will not destroy the sense of God's power but rather bolster it, but a despairing acknowledgment of our weakness will injure our sense of God's power and prevent it from working in our lives.

When human weakness is filtered through true humility, God's power is commended to the servant, accelerating the ministry's success for God. But when human weakness is filtered through a diseased form of humility, the servant commends himself to other people, and this causes the draining of God's power and the loss of the service and the pastoral spirit.

Therefore, when the priest or servant flaunts his weaknesses before the flock, whether for good reason or not, he does his calling a

---

4   It is necessary here to warn every person not to go too far in analyzing their transgressions and moral lapses and to avoid too much rumination on their sins with excessive self-reproach. Such behavior will afflict the emotions and unnecessarily weigh down the conscience, which in turn can disturb one's psychological balance. This may lead to all sorts of neuroses, which will make the person's inner healing difficult or, in rare cases, impossible.

In contrast, the spiritual and authentic method of facing one's sins in Christianity relies on the rebukes of the Holy Spirit that come without causing inward commotion: "And when He [the Holy Spirit] has come, He will convict the world of sin" (John 16:8). Therefore, he who wishes to properly examine his sins must first examine the Word of God, for the greater our knowledge of God becomes, the greater the knowledge of our sin. [Author's footnote] disservice. It is enough for a person to be humble in deed, not merely in word. The priest or servant who intentionally displays his weaknesses before his flock makes two errors:

First, he may be attempting to garner their pity or praise. Second, he may be sowing despair in their hearts, shaking their trust in God, and depriving them of a living model who was their guide.

The priest or servant is not called upon to preach *himself* or to make an exhibition of his own sins; he is called upon to preach *Christ* and is given the mandate to exhibit *His* power, a power that moves the service and from which the servant derives his faith, strength, and life.

3. It Is Better to Fall under the Yoke Than to Cast It Off

How splendid is the soldier who falls on the battlefield with his wounds still bleeding and his hands firmly grasping the weapon! His wounds tell the story of his courageous fight, and the hands still grasping his weapon bear witness to his loyalty and to the honor of his service. But the battlefield of spiritual service is incomparably greater, for the soldier who is enlisted in Christ's army does not die just once, but "for Your sake we are killed all day long" (Rom. 8:36), and we are "in deaths often" (2 Cor. 11:23).

The priest or servant appointed himself a sacrifice the day he was appointed a minister: "We are counted as sheep for the slaughter" (Ps. 44:22). So, do not condemn the fiery and poisonous arrows the enemy relentlessly shoots at your body and mind, for even if they are intended to kill, they will actually produce life: "For we who live are always delivered to death for Jesus' sake, that the life of Jesus may also be manifested in our mortal flesh" (2 Cor. 4:11).

Therefore, do not panic when you are wounded, nor be afraid of the war as though you were about to lose, for as long as your hand firmly grasps eternal life, you can never lose. Never let your hand loosen its grip on the Lord, never allow your mouth to cease crying out to Him, and never look back. For He is coming immediately, and He is coming for your deliverance. Remember that God shows great mercy to the servant who has fallen beneath his yoke, while the mercy He shows to the one who runs from his yoke is small.

4. The Yoke of Service Is Both a Mercy and a Weight

Firstly, this yoke is a kind of *mercy*, because it has called you to its service, and with the call to service necessarily comes a position of election and love: "And I thank Christ Jesus our Lord who has enabled me, because He counted me faithful, putting *me* into the ministry" (1 Tim. 1:12). Together with the call comes a plan for justification and glorification: "Moreover whom He predestined, these He also called; whom He called, these He also justified; and whom He justified, these He also glorified" (Rom. 8:30). Therefore, the service is a guarantee of mercy and a path to justification.

The servant does not justify himself, nor do his people justify him, but God does. He is the servant's righteousness. The servant may remain unrighteous in his own eyes and consider himself as nothing, but the Apostle Paul continues the verse: "What then shall we say to these things? If God *is* for us, who *can be* against us?" (Rom. 8:31). Thus, the servant receives his justification, strength, and deliverance from judgment by virtue of his appointment by God to the service. To put it differently, the service is the state in which the servant finds himself as a result of his attachment to God. In short, Christian service is a call to receive mercy and justification from God.

Secondly, this yoke is a heavy weight, but it is a weight of love. I have happily accepted this weight in honor of Him who called me. I did it by compulsion, for I was compelled by His love for me and by my love for Him. He preceded me in love by accepting this weight for me when He confirmed my salvation by His blood, washed my feet by His humility, and was pleased to pay the price of death for my liberation. And now that I have received the weight of ministry for Him, I have no right to request a reward: "Necessity is laid upon me; yes, woe is me if I do not preach the gospel!" (1 Cor. 9:16). This is how the service has become to me both a mercy and a weight: a mercy of justification imputed by God (but of which I cannot boast) and a weight of love that pulls me toward itself (and which I can never abandon).

5. The Yoke Is Both Light and Heavy

When we are in a nimble and active spiritual state, we feel the yoke of service as extremely light. Conversely, when we enter a lazy state of carelessness and shirk our proper duties, we become easily distracted, and our spiritual horizon contracts. As a result, we throw our ministry into the arms of our reason, and it becomes such an odious burden that we can scarcely tolerate it. These two states—the yoke as light and heavy—usually alternate with each other during the course of one's service, according to the relative diligence or laziness of the servant.

I will not be remiss in saying and often repeating this confession: every heaviness we feel in carrying the yoke of service is the result of our own negligence and pride!

Therefore, do not blame anyone else for the heaviness that afflicts you nor for the weight that so bitterly repels you. Look instead for the solution. There is no way to be delivered from such a burdensome yoke except by doubling one's prayer and by taking refuge in a humble life. For then the blindfold will be lifted, and in the midst of your prayer, and from the dust of your floor, you will begin to glimpse the real lightness of your yoke, and your joy and pleasure will be renewed. *And it will be the same yoke you always bore.*

6. I Have Made You a Sign

There is a task that the priest and Christian servant must accomplish, of which very few people are aware, but which is of monumental importance. They must be used by God as an example, model, or sign to the congregation. The Old Testament is of course replete with such signs, and one of the strangest of them is God's command to Ezekiel to lie on his side for 390 days, during which time God infused in him a special measure of patience to complete his prophetic ministry, which included the act of eating befouled bread. This act was meant to be a prophetic symbol of Israel's eventual fall because of its unclean sins, and the length of days would be equal to the number of years of their downfall. Later, God ordered Ezekiel to cut his hair and to throw a third of it in the fire, which was a symbol of the withdrawal of God's mercy and sustenance from Israel, their dispersion throughout the world, and their fall under the fire of God's wrath.

But in the Apostle Paul we find a new example. He says regarding himself, "For this reason I obtained mercy, that in me first Jesus Christ might show all longsuffering, as a pattern to those who are going to believe on Him for everlasting life" (1 Tim. 1:16). This is how grace works in every priest chosen by God and in every servant filled with the Holy Spirit. His presence, his words, and his life become a symbol to the congregation even without his knowing it. Grace focuses its spotlight at a special angle to bring his life into better view, whether it be his meekness, simplicity, tears, kindness, compassion, sanctity, longsuffering, sacrificial nature, or even the surrender of his whole life. Grace must sometimes employ the fires of trial and suffering to reveal these things in him—in much the same way that fire brings out the fragrant aroma of incense.

The amazing thing is that at the very moment when the priest or servant decides that he is good for nothing except the trash heap—being certain that the trials that have assailed him are the result of his sins and the just rebuke of God—grace finally accomplishes its plan. At that moment, the fire makes contact with the incense to release the aroma of Christ hidden within. And so from the very weakness the servant so despises in himself arises the grace that becomes a sign of God's mercy. If the servant, wallowing in grief over his weakness, would only open his dejected ears to hear God's opinion on the matter, he would hear these words: "It is because of your weakness that I have chosen you to be a sign of My mercy."

7. Both Sufficient and Insufficient

It is crucial that a servant see himself as unfitting or insufficient for the service—although, at the same time, he must realize that he plays a necessary role in that service. For though the salvation of a human soul is not the work of man, it nevertheless is achieved *through* man. Therefore, despite the fact that the servant should never make the error of seeing himself as a "savior," he must know that he is still a *means* or *instrument* of salvation.

As the Apostle Paul says, "Who *is* sufficient for these things?" (2 Cor. 2:16). In other words, who is in charge of the life and death of others? He says a little later: "You are our epistle written in our hearts, known and read by all men; clearly you are an epistle of Christ, ministered by us, written not with ink but by the Spirit of the living God. . . . Not that we are sufficient of ourselves to think of anything as *being* from ourselves, but our sufficiency *is* from God, who also made us sufficient as ministers of the new covenant" (2 Cor. 3:2, 3, 5, 6). When the servant is thus firmly convinced of the sufficiency given to him by God, it is one of the greatest indicators that his service will be successful in giving glory to God.

8. Helpful Praise versus Harmful Praise

There are three types of praise that the servant encounters. The first two are detrimental, but the third is beneficial.

The first is that which the servant ascribes to himself in his own conscience. It causes damage by making a sort of scandal of his whole service, for it becomes clear that his deeds are done not for God's glory but for the ego's: "For not he who commends himself is approved, but whom the Lord commends" (2 Cor. 10:18). The second is the praise other people bestow on him, but without God's guidance or approval. This form of praise must also be rejected, because it injures the service by removing the honor and glory that are due solely to God and ascribing them to the servant. As a result, both the servant and his service start to deteriorate, "whose praise *is* not from men but from God" (Rom. 2:29).

The third type of praise is that which proceeds from God Himself. This type of praise is spoken by Him into the hearts of the servant's friends and hearers, so that their hearts and consciences are stirred to confess God's favor upon him: "[We are] not walking in craftiness nor handling the word of God deceitfully, but by manifestation of the truth commending ourselves to every man's conscience *in the sight of God*" (2 Cor. 4:2, emphasis added). Such praise redounds to God Himself and turns into a proclamation of the work He has done in His people. The Apostle Paul states this very clearly: "But with me it is a very small thing that I should be judged by you or by a human court. In fact, I do not even judge myself. For I know of nothing against myself, yet I am not justified by this; but He who judges me is the Lord. Therefore judge nothing before the time, until the Lord comes, who will both bring to light the hidden things of darkness and reveal the counsels of the hearts. Then each one's praise will come from God" (1 Cor. 4:3–5). Paul also warns his congregation against superfluous praise that does not come by inspiration of God:

"Now these things, brethren, I have figuratively transferred to myself and Apollos for your sakes, that you may learn in us not to think beyond what is written, that none of you may be puffed up on behalf of one against the other" (1 Cor. 4:6).

The servant who receives the praise of God that is channeled through the hearts and consciences of others never really detects this praise. Neither does he feel that anything he says or does (no matter how influential) renders him worthy of such praise. Moses could not see the light emanating from his face, but the people saw it clearly and feared, to the point that Moses was compelled to cover his face with a veil so the people would not behold the surpassing glory. That event indeed prefigured the light that shines from Christ's own face, which we must behold in the Gospel as well as in the faces of those who read and serve the Gospel. This light is seen by the heart as Christ's truth, which reveals the sins and impurities that are concealed within.

Therefore, every servant who faithfully looks toward the light of Christ's face (which is the *truth* residing in the Word of Life) necessarily changes into the very nature of that light. As the Apostle Paul says, "Nevertheless when one turns to the Lord, the veil is taken away. . . . But we all, with unveiled face, beholding as in a mirror the glory of the Lord, are being transformed into the same image from glory to glory, just as by the Spirit of the Lord" (2 Cor. 3:16, 18). All the glory of the service is from first to last the same as Christ's glory: "For it is the God who commanded light to shine out of darkness, who has shone in our hearts to *give* the light of the knowledge of the glory of God in the face of Jesus Christ" (2 Cor. 4:6).

9. Changes in the Servant's Character

He who takes up the yoke of service as one who is consecrated and set apart no longer retains the rights that other people have, such as enjoyment of bodily ease, indulgence in temporal pleasures, and submission to the delights of nature. The cow that has taken up the yoke and been assigned to the work of plowing and tillage can no longer produce milk like the rest of the cows, who live easily on the pasture with no duties except to eat and sleep. Its supply of milk drastically decreases as it bends its knees to the work and develops the musculature to fit the needs of its particular service, and it will never again calve.

In the same way, when the human servant takes up his yoke, he will often murmur in the beginning at the deprivation of the natural rights he once enjoyed. But after a certain amount of time, his soul begins to detach from its dependency on them. Eventually, he rises completely above them, no longer feeling deprived of anything at all. In fact, he gains a strong sense of blessing, divine help, and spiritual consolation that prove to be far better than anything he had in the world. The weight of the burden of God's service, when joined to faithfulness and patience, is sufficient to bring about mighty changes in the essential being, nature, and desires of the human person.

10. *Death and Life*

One of the foundational principles for the servant who has taken up the yoke and surrendered his life to God is expressed by the Apostle Paul in these words: "Death is working in us, but life in you" (2 Cor. 4:12). In another place, he expresses it thus: "I will very gladly spend and be spent for your souls" (2 Cor. 12:15). And he says it most clearly here: "We who live are always delivered to death for Jesus' sake, that the life of Jesus also may be manifested in our mortal flesh" (2 Cor. 4:11).

These words are profoundly important, because they are, in short, a practical picture of the work of the Cross, which Christ voluntarily accepted by becoming weak while at the same time being strong.

We earlier called this a foundational principle in service, because it is Christ Himself who created it and furthermore carried it out to fulfillment in His life: "Unless a grain of wheat falls into the ground and dies, it remains alone; but if it dies, it produces much grain" (John 12:24). St. Paul also picks up on this thought and develops it into a theological concept: "If One died for all, then all died; and He died for all, that those who live should live no longer for themselves, but for Him who died for them and rose again" (2 Cor. 5:14, 15).

In the servant's mind, his soul and body are pressed and exhausted by the yoke of service, since it is a type of cross. And this "death" that he voluntarily undergoes—by frequent vigils, fasts, prayers, asceticism, and his constant concern about the people he serves—proceeds simultaneously with the involuntary death that comes from disease, want, hardship, persecution, and the rest of those things to which there seems to be no solution or alternative.

But this "dual death," both voluntary and involuntary, is in no way superfluous, for it is death unto the Lord. It is a cross-like death (that is, patterned on the Lord's death on the Cross), from which comes resurrection and new life, characterized by the same power and depth as our Lord's resurrection and life. And this occurs not merely to the appointed servant of the people but to any person who prays for them, suffers for them, loses sleep so that they might rest, fasts in their place, or repents in their name. Just as the Lord's death redounded to His own glory and gave life to those for whom He died, so also those who die in love and honor for Christ's sake work for the redemption of sinners.

11. An Unstable Mind versus a Sound Mind

There is another important principle of Christian service which, if neglected, will cause the yoke on our necks to grow heavier and our souls to shrivel up. St. Paul summarizes the principle in the following way: "If we are beside ourselves, *it is* for God; or if we are of sound mind, *it is* for you" (2 Cor. 5:13). The proclamation of the Gospel will seem to many to be unbelievable and even illogical. The idea of a crucified God cannot be understood or appreciated by people living in darkness, because they do not realize the gravity of sin or its fatal effect on the soul. Hence the world rejects purity, because it does not know the source of its power; the glutton loathes fasting; and those who are addicted to their desires cannot see the vital importance of both to their souls, because they live according to the flesh and not according to the spirit. In the same way, those who dress modestly, are well mannered, and use only appropriate speech are often harassed by those who live a loose and permissive lifestyle, who simply obey their biological drives, and who live for money to display their bodies. Likewise, the virtues of true humility and unfeigned meekness are spurned by the proud in heart and by those whose main ambition is fame and glory.

Thus, the more the servant of God and the preacher of the Spirit is faithful and exacting in his proclamation of the Gospel, the more will he be considered mad or unstable (and will be aggressively criticized) by the judgmental, the licentious, the educated, and the "wise" of this world, who calculate and decide everything by the laws of the natural order.

If the servant does not from the outset accept that he will be considered crazy or senseless in the eyes of such people, receiving it as a matter of course, he will inevitably suffer an inward schism, especially if he attempts to appear logical to these scoffers and braggarts. He will then fall victim to hypocrisy, denying the true, spiritual, and saving state of the spirit which alone heals the natural and logical mind. If such harsh judgments are unavoidable for the faithful servant, he must remember that he is "out of his mind" for God's own sake. By the same token, if the servant is considered to be of sound mind by the children of light who seek the face of God, then he is right-minded for them and not for himself, for God does not grant a servant wisdom, eloquence, or spiritual vision to benefit himself, but to benefit others: "God [pleads] through us" (2 Cor. 5:20).

12. The Justified Sinner

There is another great principle that guides the life of a servant, which reveals to him all the vistas of Christian service in their complete length and width, and grants him a bold and undisturbed conscience. This principle separates his current life from his past life, especially if his past was full of sin and errors. This principle is simply that the former servant of the flesh has now become a new creation in Christ.

We may broaden our understanding of this notion extensively if we consult the practical and faith-inspired theology of St. Paul, which he gleaned by experiencing it firsthand. He says that due to Christ's work, in God's sight we are no longer what we used to be: "Old things have passed away" (2 Cor. 5:17). For Christ, by His heroic love and His divine body, has fused His people corporately into His Person, as well as into His resurrected life: "The love of Christ compels us" (2 Cor. 5:14). We died with Christ when He died for us, we rose with Him, and we are now risen in Him: "If One died for all, then all died" (2 Cor. 5:14). Now we no longer live for ourselves or according to our old selves, "that those who live should live no longer for themselves, but for Him who died for them and rose again" (2 Cor. 5:15). Our first selves died, and in Christ we have now become new selves: "Behold, all things have become new" (2 Cor. 5:17). Our initial traits are no longer reckoned, our initial sins are no longer counted, "not imputing their trespasses to them" (2 Cor. 5:19).

Therefore, since we are servants no longer defined by our old traits, and since we do not stand before God in our former fleshly clothing, it is essential that we come to fully know about this new appearance that has been created in us by the Spirit and in the grace and truth that are in Christ: "If anyone *is* in Christ, *he is* a new creation" (2 Cor. 5:17). We are now also deemed through Christ to be justified by our heavenly Father: "We [are] the righteousness of God in Him" (2 Cor. 5:21). For we are His handiwork, His redeemed, and the fruit of His cross. Furthermore, since we have been spiritually clothed in Him, our old selves are hidden from God's sight, and the life we now live, we no longer live for ourselves or for the sake of the flesh, but Christ Himself lives in us by the Spirit. The most important goal of our life now is not to serve ourselves but rather to serve Him who died for us and rose again by the Spirit and for this living faith.

By virtue of this life-giving truth, the Christian servant can lift his eyes from what was his previous focal point (himself) and resolutely fix his eyes, heart, and mind on Christ's face. He need never look back until he is transformed by the Spirit into a new man, with a new image, into the likeness of Christ Himself, from glory to glory! Here is the essential point: the Christian servant serves Christ, not himself; therefore, he should not drag behind him the weight of his sins and his past life, nor the weight of his present weakness. Rather, he serves by Christ's righteousness; he speaks by Christ's righteousness; and he counsels and exhorts by Christ's righteousness. "He made Him who knew no sin *to be* sin for us, that we might become the righteousness of God in Him" (2 Cor. 5:21).

CHAPTER 7

Stumbling Blocks for the Christian Servant

When an average believer lags in the spiritual life and fails to display the courage that is natural to faith in Christ, neglecting to pay the "kingdom tax" that is required of him (which sometimes entails his own death), his failure is limited to his own life and is his personal responsibility. But when a priest or servant fails in some aspect of spiritual life, the effects of the failure touch not only himself but also many other aspects of the Christian service. This is because the servants' actions wield a considerable influence over the faith of the weak, as well as over the faith of their coworkers in the apostolic mission. The end result of this detrimental process is that the blame gets shifted from the servant to the service and ultimately to the Lord of the service Himself.

When we speak here of personal stumbling blocks, we are not referring to the common weaknesses of spiritual life that afflict humanity in general, such as the love of money or position, pride, anger, or lying. Nor do we mean bad habits like alcoholism, drugs, or any toxic traits that characterize a degenerate lifestyle, for these are not the stumbling blocks of a Christian servant but of a person who has not advanced past the stage of a catechumen.

Rather, the stumbling blocks of Christian service are "specialized"—that is, they are directly connected to the nature and circumstances of the service. As soon as St. Paul says, "We give no offense in anything, that our ministry might not be blamed," he immediately defines the source and nature of such offenses one by one: "But in all *things* we commend ourselves as ministers of God: in much patience, in tribulations, in needs, in distresses, in stripes, in imprisonments, in tumults, in labors, in sleeplessness, in fastings; by purity, by knowledge, by longsuffering, by kindness, by the Holy Spirit, by sincere love, by the word of truth" (2 Cor. 6:3–7).

1. *Lack of Patience*

"We commend ourselves as ministers of God: in much patience" (2 Cor. 6:4). The Christian servant may be tempted to lose his patience as a result of the setbacks that normally occur in the work itself, or as a result of the carelessness or evasiveness of the people he serves, or their lack of "ears to hear" sound teaching and rebuke.

If the servant loses his patience in such cases, he risks destabilizing the service, choking those talents that lead to the spread of the Gospel. Moreover, lack of patience is a painful blow to evangelism and faith, because it inherently points to a lack of faith. Unfortunately, the blame for this process gets transferred from the servant himself to the Church at large, and its power and work fall into disrepute. Therefore, it is a thousand times better for the servant to deliver his testimony to the people all day long, enduring the difficulties and setbacks he encounters with the utmost patience till the day he dies, than for him to throw off the yoke and flee from it, thereby weakening the credibility and confidence of the service.

We should never forget that this is an extremely common

stumbling block in Christian service; indeed, the Apostle Paul had to face it many times in himself, which he did with a firm and dauntless courage: "For we do not want you to be ignorant, brethren, of our trouble which came to us in Asia: that we were burdened beyond measure, above strength, so that we despaired even of life. Yes, we had the sentence of death in ourselves. . . . Our bodies had no rest, but we were troubled on every side. Outside *were* conflicts, inside *were* fears. Nevertheless God, who comforts the downcast, comforted us" (2 Cor. 1:8, 9; 7:5, 6). We should remember the importance of the words "much patience" that St. Paul uses to describe his service.

2. *The Fear of Hardship*

The yoke of service does not primarily consist in sharing calm and happy words, in comfortable evangelism, or in easy teaching. Instead, it is primarily and fundamentally *war*. It is war against the powers of darkness, because sinful and careless souls are easy prey for deceitful spirits, and such evil spirits seize control of their minds by deceptive and ruthless devices. Therefore, the Christian servant is inevitably bound to meet these powers face to face. They use hidden snares and terrifying attacks against the servant. For example, they rouse against him evil people and authorities, who work to impede his progress; they plague him with doubt; and they confuse people's thoughts regarding his motives and opinions.

Hence, strife and conflict are a necessary part of Christian service, since it is the act of freeing sinners from the bonds of the satanic powers. Christian service is a direct opposition and enmity to the powers of darkness. If the servant's own strength falters in the conflict and he surrenders in the fight, especially in the beginning of his service (no matter how good the reason), he strips the service bare and exposes it. Therefore, it is of the utmost importance for the servant to reconcile himself to a life of longsuffering, struggle, persistence, patience, and a resolution never to waver in the face of the enemy's attacks, even if it means death! St. Paul speaks to the servants and preachers of the Gospel with the following words of warning and encouragement:

> Finally, my brethren, be strong in the Lord and in the power of His might. Put on the whole armor of God, that you may be able to stand against the wiles of the devil. For we do not wrestle against flesh and blood, but against principalities, against powers, against the rulers of the darkness of this age, against spiritual *hosts* of wickedness in the heavenly *places*. Therefore take up the whole armor of God, that you may be able to withstand in the evil day, and having done all, to stand.
>
> Stand therefore, having girded your waist with truth, having put on the breastplate of righteousness, and having shod your feet with the preparation of the gospel of peace; above all, taking the shield of faith with which you will be able to quench all the fiery darts of the wicked one. And take the helmet of salvation, and the sword of the Spirit, which is the word of God; praying always with all prayer and supplication in the Spirit, being watchful to this end with all perseverance and supplication. (Eph. 6:10–18)

3. *The Fear of Harsh Inevitabilities*

St. Paul speaks of three different types of urgent conditions, or inevitable states of want or need the Christian servant should expect to encounter:

+ harsh conditions of nature, such as heat, cold, rain, storm, desert, mountains, and roaming beasts;
+ lack of access to things needed by the body or for everyday life

(whether for himself, his family, or his church), which produces
hunger, thirst, cold, and lack of rest;
+ the realities of disease and suffering.

These various inevitabilities will come to meet the Christian servant
repeatedly during his journey through life, and he must take it as a
certainty that he will eventually confront them as blunt facts of existence. There will be no way to solve them except to realize that these
events do not occur needlessly or haphazardly, but by God's permission. As such, they should be weighed on the scale of the servant's
personal crown of salvation. (The devil, on the other hand, exper-
iments with these conditions to test their effectiveness as weapons
against mankind and employs them in unforeseeable and sudden
ways which leave no room for doubt that they are part of his ruthless
battle against us.)

Therefore, if the servant is stricken with terror at meeting such
circumstances and fails to use his only weapon of prayer, he may
resort to illegitimate means of coping with these difficulties, such as
employing bribery, flattery, or threats against others, or merely seeking a way of escape. When the servant is found in a state like this, the
devil increases the violence and menace of his attacks to strike fear
into his heart, with the hope that the servant will cast away his weapons altogether and abandon the battleground of service, covered with
shame and humiliation. In fact, all such urgent and terrifying situations are nothing more than the firing of empty blanks—things any
person can face directly and expose them for the hollow and power-
less phantoms they are.

The extremities of nature, the needs of the body, and disease and
pain can all be transformed by the Holy Spirit of God into fundamental means for the success of Christian service and the revelation
of God's glory, but only if the servant is able to remain steadfast
through them, accept them with thanksgiving, and pass through

them until the end with a smile. God is always glorified in a special way in such distressing circumstances, even when the night of trials appears to be endless. The stories of God's deeds among His saints in times of difficulty and want are manifold and encouraging.

One of the most dangerous falls a servant of God can suffer is a desire for increase in money and wealth as a safeguard for the future:

> Now godliness with contentment is great gain. For we brought nothing into *this* world, *and it is* certain we can carry nothing out. And having food and clothing, with these we shall be content. But those who desire to be rich fall into temptation and a snare, and *into* many foolish and harmful lusts which drown men in destruction and perdition. For the love of money is a root of all *kinds of* evil, for which some have strayed from the faith in their greediness, and pierced themselves through with many sorrows. (1 Tim. 6:6–10)

4. Failure to Bear Hardship

The general predicament to which St. Paul constantly alludes is when a servant feels besieged on all sides by difficulties and is placed in circumstances much more challenging than he is capable of handling—whether physical, psychological, mental, or even spiritual. In such situations, the ghost of past failures comes to frighten him. He looks for help from any other human being but finds none, and he loses all confidence in himself and in his ability to endure anything. The mind of a person in such a state becomes squeezed into the narrowest of mental straits, and he loses hope as he sees failure visibly approaching him. This is the conflict of faith, the conflict of hope; and it is a time to cleave firmly to the promises of God.

Since a person in this unfortunate state can scarcely be a witness to God or His service, the devil enters and prods him to curse his failings and abandon his faith. But the power of God's help is ready to help him stand, and a promised door of victory stands before him, but it can be opened only if he once and for all decides to take hold of living hope and to defy the odds. The salvation that God promises to those who struggle in His name requires a faith much greater than normal. Indeed, it must be a faith to guide him through utter darkness.

A Christian servant must know from the outset and understand very well that from the very first hour of his service, the enemy will begin to collect evidence against him and will preserve it for a specific moment. And at the time of the servant's trial, he suddenly presents it to the servant to make the darkness seem impenetrable and as a proof from his past behavior that his failure is guaranteed and that retreat is a very reasonable option.

O servant, stand firm, stay calm, and remain patiently resolute in your goals until you pass through the hour of darkness and put an end to the bragging cheers of the evil power. In that hour, you will see the enemy broken, and you will rejoice and glorify the victory you gained in the One you love, who first loved you. In that moment, remember this saying of the Apostle Paul: "For God has not given us a spirit of fear, but of power and of love and of a sound mind" (2 Tim. 1:7).

5. Breaking Down under Attack

The apostles and preachers of old were often struck by rods on their naked bodies by their persecutors, who tried to crush their physical strength by the force of the blows, to crush their mental endurance by humiliation, and ultimately to cause them to abandon the faith and become apostates. This has been the devil's scheme from the very beginning, and he even attempted to carry it out against Christ in Gethsemane: "I will strike the Shepherd, and the sheep will be scattered" (Mark 14:27).

Although the devil has now changed the manner of his attacks, he has not ceased to attack. His blows are just as hard and frequent, but they come in the form of discrimination, slander, and abuse. The humiliation he imposes comes by the distortion and complication of truth. To injure the soul is a thousand times better for him than to injure the body. The devil's ultimate goal is to destroy the servant's strength and motivation by endlessly torturing his soul, so that he finally flees the battleground of service and escapes the critics, slanderers, and devils that threaten him.

The apostles taught us about this necessary state of affairs after they were first taught by grace. For when they were charged by the Sanhedrin and beaten with rods, they went out rejoicing, and their souls were unshaken by the humiliation, because they counted all their sufferings as worthy of Christ's name. Therefore, we say that every humiliation and slander we receive in bearing Christ's yoke is counted as a sacrifice offered to honor Christ's name; indeed, it is truly a sharing in Christ's own sacrifice. "Remember Jesus Christ . . . for [whom] I suffer trouble as an evildoer, *even* to the point of chains" (2 Tim. 2:8, 9).

> I was appointed a preacher, an apostle, and a teacher of the Gentiles. For this reason I also suffer these things; nevertheless I am not ashamed, for I know whom I have believed and am persuaded that He is able to keep what I have committed to Him until that Day. Therefore do not be ashamed of the testimony of our Lord, nor of me His prisoner, but share with me in the sufferings for the gospel according to the power of God. (2 Tim. 1:11, 12, 8)

6. *Flight from Prison*

Prison stifles a person's soul so much that his hope becomes strangled, he surrenders to fate, and he gives up his duty to proclaim the Gospel. But a person can be imprisoned in mind without being imprisoned in body. When a servant's diligence and evangelism are "arrested"—that is, when his words and deeds are under constant scrutiny or when he is prohibited from communicating with the children he serves, with his disciples, or with the sick—these are but modern forms of imprisonment. Now, if the servant refuses to accept such circumstances and to work within the limitations and bonds placed upon him, his soul will tear itself apart. His mind will implode, and his nerves will become utterly frayed. In the end, he will abandon himself to grumbling and complaining, which will only cause him to be further marginalized and confined. Finally, he will abandon the arena of service to the wanton and the corrupt.

The point we must bear in mind is that imprisonment, in all its different forms, has been a hallmark of Christian service since the days of the apostles. It remains so, even until this day. Therefore, it is our duty to accept the bonds and chains associated with it, whether visible or invisible, whether physical, psychological, or emotional. (This is only one way the people of the world use to resist the servants and evangelists of the Gospel.) It is also critical that we understand the fact that resigning ourselves to complaining and anxiety on account of the negative feelings associated with such chains is enough to make a person succumb to mental division and internal revolt. This inevitably leads to a denial of the service, damage to the honored Name, and shame to the preaching of the cross.

Dear servant, remember the chains by which Christ was bound and to which He submitted, even to the point of the cross! And remember St. Paul, the ambassador in chains, who deemed his removal from confinement in Judea to his imprisonment in Rome (while bound with chains) the highest form of ambassadorship for the sake of Christ's service. His was a chained mission. And how splendid, how wonderful were those chains! St. John Chrysostom once said that if he could choose any one of St. Paul's many gifts to take for himself, he would choose his chains.

7. Cowardice in the Face of Troubles

The troubles we encounter can be either contrived or natural. The former occurs when the devil stirs up uproars and tumults against the Christian servant, as in the case of the pandemonium that broke out in Ephesus during the visit of the Apostle Paul. The entire city was in an uproar, led by the chief manufacturer of small idols of the goddess Artemis. The mob shouted frantically while throwing dust into the air, all in protest against Paul, who ostensibly had come to ruin their business and overthrow their pagan worship. The adversary orchestrates such revolts to strike fear in the heart of the servant and to terrify him into taking flight.

Natural troubles are those that are a natural consequence of living in times of war, revolution, famine, or natural disasters. At such times, the adversary applies extra pressure on the heart and mind of the servant to weaken him and stop him from speaking the truth in God's service. Alternately, the servant might choose his own safety by fleeing, forsaking his flock and exposing it to division and harm. However, how vital is the need for someone to lead them through such storms, to guide them through dangerous passages, to pray for them, and to humble himself enough to experience their troubles with them! In such perilous times, the true shepherd is distinguished from the hireling, for the latter flees for his life and does not scruple to abandon the flock to destruction.

8. Relaxing When Struggle Is Needed

The farmer who diligently attends to the demands and seasons of his occupation must be a stranger to sloth and relaxation, whether he is plowing his land, sowing seed, or harvesting the crop. For if he loses focus and becomes lazy, either he will miss the season, or his seed will go bad, or his crop will fail. His bare and miserable field tells an eloquent story of his cheap laziness and sad carelessness. He will be able neither to supply the wants of the public nor to provide for his own needs.

When a church on Sundays and feast days is empty of believers, it is precisely in the same state. Its emptiness tells an eloquent story of the negligence of its shepherd and servants, who have forsaken their spiritual service, who have gone to sow their seed in the ocean and to reap their crop in the wind. How sad and how shameful! However, this is only a foretaste of the scene that will occur before the judgment seat of Christ, when those who have been endowed with gifts and entrusted with the stewardship of the holy mysteries will stand guilty of having squandered the gifts or exploited them for monetary gain.

The servant's true rest awaits him in heaven with his Lord, who also needed to suffer before entering into His rest. We will not find our true rest here. Christ's own hands hold it in a large vessel in heaven. As the Apostle Paul states, "And to whom did He swear that they would not enter His rest, but to those who did not obey? . . . Therefore, since a promise remains of entering His rest, let us fear lest any of you seem to have come short of it. . . . Let us therefore be diligent to enter that rest, lest anyone fall according to the same example of disobedience" (Heb. 3:18; 4:1, 11). We live in the time of labor and exhaustion, as St. Paul says: "Our bodies [have] no rest" (2 Cor. 7:5). However, the labor is holy and worthy, because it produces the fruits of peace and eternal salvation. This labor will cause the face of God's shepherd and servant to shine with glory before Him: "Those who understand shall shine like the brightness of the firmament, and some who are righteous, like the stars of heaven forever and ever" (Dan. 12:3 OSB).

9. Sleep When Vigilance Is Required

Christ's heart was seared by the sight of His disciples sleeping during the most distressing hour of His life. They were asleep at the time when wakefulness and vigilance were most needed, and Christ made three attempts to rouse them. They slept, even though He warned them to "rise and pray, lest you enter into temptation" (Luke 22:46). In the parable of the vigilant servant (Luke 12:35–40), He warns our hearts that whenever the devil sees an inattentive mind, he sneaks into the house of the spiritual man to steal, pillage, and lay waste whatever he had stored up by the sweat of his prayers and by the tears of his repentance.

A crafty wolf does not attack a flock of sheep that is supervised by an alert and vigilant shepherd, but it makes its round of several different flocks until it finds one whose shepherd lies on the ground with a blanket covering him and has fallen into a deep slumber. In such an instance, the wolf has found a favorable opportunity to attack and disperse the sheep.

The watchful priest never allows his church to be invaded. Neither does he ever overlook a single sheep or even the smallest lamb, for he is ready to give his life for the youngest of his sheep. He pours out his entire life for them because he knows that it is stored up and guarded for him ultimately in heaven. If he loses his life for Christ's sake, he will receive it back from Him in heaven, crowned with glory. But if he covers his face and goes to sleep or abandons the sheep to avoid danger for himself, he destroys his soul, surrendering it to a judgment that is without mercy, and he enters into an eternal desolation.

The Christian priest or servant is therefore a guardian of sheep before being a preacher or instructor. The lost lambs will be required of him, and the blood of those that are killed is on his hands.

10. *Neglect of Fasting*

A stomach that is overstuffed with food and pampered with exquisite treats will not produce a spiritual person. Fasting and prayer are necessary forms of spiritual suffering for the shepherd, for through them Christ's image becomes revealed in his newly created children: "My little children, for whom I labor in birth again until Christ is formed in you . . . in weariness and toil, in sleeplessness often, in hunger and thirst, in fastings often, in cold and nakedness" (Gal. 4:19; 2 Cor. 11:27). When a person adorns the temple of his heart with fasting and prayer, it becomes a natural dwelling place for the Holy Spirit, and the stomach immediately loses its dominance over the person. Conversely, if he pampers his stomach with delectable items, the stomach will seize power over his entire being: "They are the enemies of the cross of Christ . . . whose god *is their* belly" (Phil. 3:18, 19).

A pastor or servant who does not participate regularly in the church fasts and spiritual austerities for the sake of himself and his service falls from his spiritual rank and can no longer remain faithful to the observances and rules of the Church. Instead, you always find him revolting against the systems of the Church and attacking its traditions, especially fasting. This form of whining and moaning goes far back in church history: "Now I urge you, brethren, note those who cause divisions and offenses, contrary to the doctrine which you learned, and avoid them. For those who are such do not serve our Lord Jesus Christ, but their own belly" (Rom. 16:17, 18). A fundamental precept of patristic ascetic wisdom, dating back centuries and still true today, is that if you want to begin to cultivate a particular virtue or to start some spiritual service, you must begin by fasting.

Thus, if the pastor or servant releases himself from fasting as a continual policy in his service, then without his realizing it, the service will degenerate from being a spiritual work to a social work, and it will gradually turn into a mere performance of human effort. It will become an arena of jokes, amusements, and parodies, and it will have no residue of the Spirit left, except for a few religious words and verses used to pacify spiritual infants.

11. Lack of Purity

How beautiful is your aroma, O priest, who have divested yourself of carnal desire![5] My brother, the scent of chastity rises from you, or rather, the fragrant aroma of Christ Himself that rises to God. Everyone who experiences your fragrance senses the power of your purity and the eternity that abides in you. How wonderful are your eyes, which remind one of the face of the Virgin or of God's own face. The innocence of eternal life that gleams from those eyes expels carnal desire from the hearts of those who behold you!

Why speak, O chaste virgin? Your appearance is sermon enough. Your presence brings forth hope. Your sitting bespeaks peace. Your smile is joy. Your tears expel sin from the bodily members! Make sure, brother, not to slacken your toil, for your glittering crown hovers above your head, held in the hands of your guardian angel, and on it is written, "Here is the patience of the saints"!

You are not alone, but you are in a great company of fellow strugglers who support you with their tears. Your sighs ring like music in the angels' ears; your pains are accounted as something precious, and your groans are a melody that delights the spirits of the righteous.

---

5   There is a tradition in the Church that was passed down until very recent times—and is likely still observed by some in our day—that the man who has finished raising his children and has been called to the priesthood ceases sexual activity. This is the remark of the church historian Socrates of Constantinople: "In the East, the priests and bishops refrain from copulating with their wives. But this they do by their own choice, for there is no canon which requires such behavior of them as a matter of necessity. In fact, there were also bishops who bore children through their wives during the period of their episcopacy." Socrates Scholasticus, *Hist. Eccl.*, v. 22.

Be strong, then, so that those who look for salvation might also be strengthened.

The Lord tied the state of the eyes to that of the whole body by His saying, "The lamp of the body is the eye. If therefore your eye is good, your whole body will be full of light" (Matt. 6:22). He made clear the starting point of a shepherd's struggle with himself. His own purity protects the purity of his service. When the eyes are "dyed" with Christ's blood, they become cleansed, purified, and sanctified, until the light of Christ emerges from them. When the mind and heart thus become an illuminated temple of the Holy Spirit, there can be no fear of their destruction. But when, conversely, the eyes are absorbed in fleshly desires, the mind becomes malleable to Satan's influence—not merely to unclean lusts but also to covetousness, scorn, and contrariness. Then the eyes become a danger at every moment. At such times, a simple bad mood of the priest or servant can strip him of his spiritual well-being, and a single look or laugh can cause harm.

The priest who has developed "unhealthy eyes" forfeits his ability and right to look after his flock. When the sheep perceive his fallen state, they may even resolve to care for *him* with prayer and fasting. Oh, how unfortunate is the priest who has squandered the health of his eyes! One may well ask if he has practically given up on his profession. The sins of other people follow after them, but the sins of the pastor and servant go before them (1 Tim 5:24). The seriousness of a sin is proportionate to the size of the ministry, and the stench of sin cannot be covered up with incense or perfumes. Indeed, the adulterous eye often has the sorrowful look of perceiving the great judgment to come!

"[Exhort] older women as mothers, younger women as sisters, with all purity" (1 Tim. 5:2).

"Keep yourself pure" (1 Tim. 5:22).

12. *Lack of Knowledge*

It is not a dishonor to God's minister to be uninformed in the natural sciences (medicine, engineering, astronomy, etc.), even though the ancient theological school of Alexandria concerned itself with such fields. It is a shame, however, for God's minister to be ignorant in ecclesiastical studies. For how can he relay the message of sound faith and doctrine with a zealous purpose if he has not studied church history? How can he teach others if he himself does not know the long wars waged by the Church against false teaching to preserve right belief and doctrine? If we but knew the amount of sweat, blood, and strife it took to settle each word of the Creed, and how much blood of the martyrs, confessors, and struggles of faith have stained past centuries in the fight, we would begin to understand how closely the Creed is bound up with our history and how worthwhile is the prolonged and attentive study of its contents!

In the same manner, one's interpretation of the Bible is linked to one's doctrine, which in turn is influenced by the school of thought one studies on a daily basis. If a priest or servant does not formulate his thoughts by the daily study of the Holy Fathers and does not lay the foundation of his theology on patristic doctrine (thereby avoiding the benefits of the correction and growth they provide), then he will be incapable of making his flock into disciples of the truth. He will be ineffective in nurturing the next generation on the firm basis of correct faith and doctrine.

A preacher or servant's negligence or even outright ignorance of patristic teaching is sufficient to create, over time, a wide and perilous chasm between believers and the doctrinal and intellectual inheritance of the Church. This, in turn, will lead to a generation utterly unfamiliar with the order and rites of the Church. Such believers will mercilessly criticize the Church, because they do not understand her spiritual heritage. "Give attention to reading. . . . Take heed to yourself and to the doctrine. Continue in them, for in doing this you will save both yourself and those who hear you" (1 Tim. 4:13, 16).

13. *Lack of Greatheartedness and Longsuffering*

The longsuffering that St. Paul requires of the Christian servant is like that of an athlete running with perseverance down a long and winding track. The servant or priest will not be able to possess the virtue of longsuffering unless he is ready to become the most abject tool in the service of his Lord's children, and no reason or excuse can cause him to shirk his duties. This comes to pass when the priest shuns thinking of himself too much and abandons the sense that he is completely independent in the service, for he is aware of his absolute subjection to the authority of his Lord Jesus. He will then have proper patience of soul toward the wayward, the scorners, and troublemakers, because he is responsible for them. He will never give up hope in any person, no matter how bad their sin, because that would mean he had given up hope in himself. He will be continually certain that as long as time exists, the door of repentance is open, and salvation's crown is always within the reach even of the worst of sinners.

However, if the servant or priest loses patience, he will become subservient to his ego and claim allegiance only to his own whim and authority, thus forsaking the worship and honorable service of the Lord Christ. He will begin to quibble with the sinners he serves, treating them not as children of his Lord but rather as his own personal attendants. He will not take offense at their disobedience to Christ, but he will take offense at their disobedience to his wounded pride. And so the service that should be spiritual turns into a personal battleground; sacrifice is replaced by personal gain; and a seemly and lowly demeanor toward fellow servants of the cross is replaced by a confrontational and threatening attitude.

The priest who abandons his service because of personal stress or due to the faults and scorn of his flock is no less dangerous than the one who mistreats them because of his wounded pride, for the minister who forsakes his flock essentially hands them over to the enemy. How needful then is longsuffering! It can be gained in no other way than by accepting the ministry as a sacred burden on the back, a burden that the servant has no right to cast off.

14. *Lack of Kindness*

The Apostle Paul considers the height of God's kindness to be not our salvation from sin by the shedding of His blood, but His going beyond that and enthroning us with Him in the heavens. For while forgiveness of sins is a mercy, enthronement in heaven is at the very heart of His transcendent kindness: "[He] raised *us* up together, and made *us* sit together in the heavenly *places* in Christ Jesus, that in the ages to come He might show the exceeding riches of His grace in *His* kindness toward us in Christ Jesus" (Eph. 2:6, 7).

Christ displayed the highest form of kindness in that He did not merely spread a message of the necessity of suffering, but He actually sat down and ate with sinners, the poor, and the destitute. And in doing so, He defined for us one of the most important aspects of Christian service, an aspect that is no less important than the cross. He showed that kindness to poor and ill souls is an integral element in God's program of salvation; moreover, it is a foundation on which we may build people's faith in the Person of Christ. We will never be able to relay the picture of Christ's kindness toward sinners without being kind to them ourselves. If we do not transmit to others the very kindness we receive from Christ, we will also be blocked from receiving it.

Any priest or servant will not be able to sit with Christ at the feast of His Kingdom if he here refuses to sit at the table of the poor or if he refuses to invite the desolate and brokenhearted to dine with him. Hence, we see why Christ said there was such a close and tight link between our visiting the sick and imprisoned and His receiving us in the Kingdom. If the ministry fails to render acts of mercy and sympathy to the poor and sorrowful, it will have failed to reflect one of the most beautiful traits of Christ Himself!

15. *Hypocritical Love*

Even if a service is energetic, zealous, and effective, if it is not motivated by a sincere love for its children, it loses its meaning and divine value. According to the judgment of the Apostle Paul as expressed in the first letter to the Corinthians (1 Cor. 13), though a servant had the ability to speak with the tongues of men and of angels, if his ministry be devoid of sincere love for the ones he serves, his service is only as useful as the bells that ring from a church tower, or as productive as a pair of cymbals aimlessly clanging together during worship. In other words, it is something that is momentarily heard and vanishes with the wind.

Again, if a Christian servant can interpret all prophecies, penetrate all mysteries, and has faith enough to move mountains but fails to love the people he serves and teaches, then his service is equal to nothing. And if the servant is filled with zeal enough to give away all his money, or even to hand over his body for burning on behalf of people, if he has no love for them, his service will be good for nothing.

From these thoughts, it becomes apparent that genuine love for the people one serves is fundamental to the spirit of Christian service. It is the source of the service's power, the source of the fervor that fuels the servant's work, and the basis of his reward. Therefore, any bit of hypocrisy in the servant's love toward his people is enough to derail the service and spoil its fruit and reward, for any defect in love is a defect in the service.

The crucial point is that our Christian service is not just some obligatory task assigned to us, or a message to be delivered, or any other act of seeming importance—but it is an obligation to love, a message of love, a commission to love, and a burden of love. And we can never really accept this except by the love with which Christ first loved us, for we have become bondservants to the kindness of His love. We serve others, for we have been taken captive by Christ's love. We are forced by that love to serve as bondservants, and we are also served by it. And we are furthermore delighted to submit to this slavery, for we gain by it, and this subjection to the service of others becomes a means of honoring His love: "For we do not preach ourselves, but Christ Jesus the Lord, and ourselves your bondservants for Jesus' sake" (2 Cor. 4:5).

Those who have become captives and bondservants of Christ's love no longer deem it an important thing to be loved by the ones they serve to the same extent that they love them—or to be loved by them at all—for the divine love that is poured into their hearts is given from above, and it does not draw its fervor from the people they serve nor from the circumstances of their service. St. Paul describes this principle with complete conviction when he says, "And I will very gladly spend and be spent for your souls; though the more abundantly I love you, the less I am loved . . . be that *as it may*" (2 Cor. 12:15, 16).

16. Truth's Exile from Our Speech

A preacher or servant should not speak words that originate with himself, but rather the words that God speaks into his heart. He should express that which he hears and learns during his prayers and hours of solitude; he must never counterfeit the words used by the children of God, as did the false prophets of old.

The truth needs no ulterior motive. Anyone who is sent by God to speak in Christ's name will speak with Christ's tongue, serve with Christ's power, and think with Christ's mind. Nothing can be called "true" in and of itself—no saying, idea, or deed—because the truth is God Himself. Anything that comes from God is necessarily true (as long as it remains unseparated from Him). Christ is the fullness of truth, for He is the Word of God—that is, God as revealed in word, thought, and deed. Anyone who lives in Christ will live, think, and speak through Him; therefore, he will live truth, think truth, and speak truth, like a man standing before God and speaking directly to Him. As the Apostle Paul wrote, "For we are not, as so many, peddling the word of God; but as of sincerity, but as from God, we speak in the sight of God in Christ" (2 Cor. 2:17).

The servant who does not speak spiritual truth, or who refuses to witness to the truth while knowing it, in reality does not serve Christ at all. He may be serving himself, a particular person, or even the devil without realizing it. This is not just a stumbling block in service, but is itself a service of stumbling blocks. Here the service moves dangerously from the realm of light to the realm of darkness. A servant may imagine that speaking the truth or witnessing to it will hurt the service, but this is only shortsightedness. Teaching the truth cannot hurt or offend anyone except those who hate the truth and are spiritually unstable. Christ Himself spoke and witnessed to the truth, but no one stumbled at it except those who insisted on rejecting it.

Of course, it is not an easy thing for a servant to speak the truth, for the price of expressing it can sometimes be death. However, the servant in such situations has no choice, for if he refuses to speak the truth, he will be considered dead already from that moment. A servant or priest is compelled to utter the truth because he must always sense God's presence and speak in God's name. He cannot help expressing the truth that he has seen and heard: "Whether it is right in the sight of God to listen to you more than to God, you judge. For we cannot but speak the things which we have seen and heard" (Acts 4:19, 20).

CHAPTER 8

The Mandatory "Taxes" Paid by the Christian Servant

There is a glorious quality to Christian service that will always be desired by lovers of the Gospel as something that stirs the heart and energizes the will. Whether the Christian servant appears in the distinguished robes of an official hierarch or in the dress of a lowly and simple layman, he moves among us as an apostle of the Lord of hosts. The fragrant aroma of Christ emanates from him wherever he goes, and the honor that surrounds him surpasses all the honors of this world. The crowns of the earth's sovereigns bow beneath the hands that bear the cross. The Bible even commands the bestowal of this honor: "Let the elders who rule well be counted worthy of double honor, especially those who labor in the word and doctrine" (1 Tim. 5:17). And Christian servants will finally receive the culmination of the honor due to their rank in the Kingdom of God: "You are those who have continued with Me in My trials. And I bestow upon you a kingdom, just as My Father bestowed *one* upon Me" (Luke 22:28, 29).

Nobody, however, can receive such honors for free. The glories that await the faithful and diligent servant come with a mandatory "tax" that may seem exorbitant from the outside. The world imposes heavy fines and penalties on those who spurn its false offers, who rejects its lusts, and who belittle the physical and mental pleasures it offers. But it imposes its heaviest and strictest penalties on those who dare to preach the Gospel, because they openly expose the lies of this world's ruler and the futility of his pleasures and diversions. The adversary's ire is also raised at these servants' exposure of death as a defeated thing (despite being intermixed with sin, the devil's most important asset) and at their constant warnings of the eternal separation from God that awaits people if they obey the wiles of the evil one. The more a servant strives diligently to ruin Satan's schemes and to save people from the potential destruction that lies before them, the more will Satan strive to have his revenge against him.

One kind of "tax" is levied on the average Christian who need worry only about himself, while another kind is levied on God's servants who toil every day to save the lost. If we wish to compare one ministry to another or to distinguish between one servant and another, we only compare them by the type and amount of "tax" that has been imposed on them by the world. The heaviness of the tax indirectly reveals the diligence invested in the service as well as how dangerous the servant appears in the devil's eyes. We find this principle clearly reflected in St. Paul's statement, "Are they ministers of Christ?—I speak as a fool—I *am* more: in labors more abundant, in stripes above measure, in prisons more frequently, in deaths often" (2 Cor. 11:23).

The taxes imposed on Christian servants can be either personal or circumstantial. The personal taxes are those used by the devil to hurt the servant himself. The intention is to sabotage the service in its entirety, and his method is to afflict the servant with a painful illness that is slow to heal, as happened to St. Paul: "And lest I should be exalted above measure by the abundance of the revelations, a thorn in the flesh was given to me, a messenger of Satan to buffet me, lest I be exalted above measure" (2 Cor. 12:7).

The "taxes of circumstance" a servant must be prepared to deal with arise from three sources:

1. **Negative thoughts** that occur in people's minds that the devil takes advantage of to cause them to assail the service. The devil may use the servant's superiors, colleagues, friends, or enemies. He may provoke in them feelings of envy, grudges, anger, calumny, and animosity toward the servant. These hostile sentiments can even become outright war against the servant, or they can take subtler forms, such as criticism or the spreading of distorted reports of his actions and statements to denigrate his reputation, integrity, or goodness.

In such cases, the servant is faced with a war that is so bitter, so crafty, so painful, and so demonic that it is impossible for him to grapple with it by his own unaided powers. The slightest mental attention paid to these assaults is enough to cause the servant to completely lose his peace and calm; furthermore, it may even cast him headlong into anxiety, sorrow, or depression. The unfortunate consequence of all this is that his service, which was so positive and fruitful, halts, and the energy that was once invested in ministry is now redirected to dealing with a conflict that is fixated on the servant's personal honor and ego.

The Apostle Paul teaches us about the weaponry that will aid the servant in fighting these battles: "by the power of God, by the armor of righteousness on the right hand and on the left" (2 Cor. 6:7). The armor of righteousness on the right hand refers to preaching the word to rebuke sinners and to console penitents, and the armor on the left hand refers to testing the compliments and flattering words directed at us, in order to silence the mouth of the enemy and to cut off this line of attack for the adversary. "Being reviled, we bless; being persecuted, we endure; being defamed, we entreat" (1 Cor. 4:12, 13). This assumes that we have accepted the insults, offenses, and slander of others totally and with a joyful heart, simply as a tax that must be paid: "You *are* distinguished, but we *are* dishonored" (1 Cor 4:10). "As deceivers, and *yet* true" (2 Cor. 6:8).

2. The second source is **the negative influences of the devil** over the servant's own mind, heart, and body. The goal is to disturb the equilibrium of the servant's thinking and actions in order to bring him into subjection to his biological drives and to stir up anger against love, despair against hope, and greed against contentment. Here, the servant starts to doubt his suitability for the service and the validity of his call to serve. The devil thus seeks to remind the servant continually of the stumbling blocks that cause him to fall, of his inherent weaknesses, all to weigh down his conscience severely enough to swallow him up in grief.

Here again St. Paul reminds us of how vital it is to take up the armor of righteousness on the right hand, so that by the promises in God's Word we might cut off all the suggestions of the devil and combat the unrest he provokes in this body of dust:

> We do not preach ourselves. . . . But we have this treasure [the Gospel of Christ] in earthen vessels [the body], that the excellence of the power may be of God and not of us. *We are* hard-pressed on every side, yet not crushed; *we are* perplexed, but not in despair; persecuted, but not forsaken; struck down, but not destroyed—always carrying about in the body the dying of the Lord Jesus, that the life of Jesus also may be manifested in our body. For we who live are always delivered to death for Jesus' sake, that the life of Jesus also may be manifested in our mortal flesh. (2 Cor. 4:5, 7–11)

Thus, we must willingly accept the assaults of Satan and bear with patience and endurance all the afflictions that he hurls at our minds, emotions, impulses, and senses. They are but taxes being paid directly to the Lord of the flock, and we must take pains to remember what Christ said regarding the devil's role in this process: "'I will strike the Shepherd, and the sheep of the flock will be scattered" (Matt. 26:31).

3. The third source is **the volatility of the natural world**, which the devil can use as a weapon to harass the servant in any part of the world where he goes. The devil may raise tempests, cause storms on the oceans, agitate beasts, insects, and microbes of the earth, and even use the shadows of the night to terrify the servant into losing strength and doubting the reality of God's help and mercy. These represent some of the most vehement battles waged by Satan against the Apostle Paul and the rest of the evangelists and church fathers in every corner and time period of the earth. "Three times I was shipwrecked; a night and a day I have been in the deep . . . *in* perils of the Gentiles, *in* perils in the city, *in* perils in the wilderness, *in* perils in the sea . . . in hunger and thirst, in fastings often, in cold and nakedness" (2 Cor. 11:25–27). The devil does not hesitate to gather all these assaults and to concentrate them into a very narrow sliver of time, especially in the early life of a servant, to finish him off before he has a chance to build up strength and to learn the true level of his endurance. However, "we are not ignorant of his devices" (2 Cor. 2:11).

Therefore, the wise servant will settle it in his mind that from the very first word he utters in his service, from the first step he takes, he will be levied galling "taxes" without a predefined limit. However, in the end, they will be felt as a miniscule amount when compared to the tremendous aid the servant will receive directly from the Holy Spirit, sometimes even before the tax is imposed. These considerations can provide us with a reliable spiritual map for our service, so that by availing ourselves of the directions it gives, we will accurately know where we stand and safely navigate our way throughout the journey.

But before anything else, we must ask ourselves this question: Has the mandatory tax that is unfailingly placed on faithful servants been placed on us? If so, of what type is it? That is, is it assessed because of the doctrine and morals we teach? Is it levied because of the activities we organize? Or is it levied against us personally, on our hearts, which is the heaviest and most grievous price to pay?

We have no choice whether to accept these taxes or not. Their payment is imperative. They must be paid immediately and with a submissive heart. They must be paid in whatever way they are imposed on us—that is, whether they are required all at once or in a series of installments over a longer period. And we must not grumble or feel shaken up by them; our hands must cling tenaciously to the plow as it makes its way toward heaven. Any attempt to evade this tax will make us into one of those sad souls who escape the narrow way and forfeit their heavenly glory.

The servant knows that as he prostrates in pain under the vehement blows of the adversary, when he pays his taxes without complaint and without protest, the world calls him weak. Welcome, very welcome is this weakness! For by it a portion of heavenly glory is reserved for us: "Of myself I will not boast, except in my infirmities" (2 Cor. 12:5). Indeed, how auspicious is this "weakness," when Christ Himself paid the tax (before we did), without ever taking His hand off the plow: "He was crucified in weakness" (2 Cor. 13:4). St. Paul even calls Him "the weakness of God" (1 Cor. 1:25).

CHAPTER 9

The Joys of the Christian Servant

The joy of the LORD is your strength. (Neh. 8:10)

1. The Joy of the Friend of the Bridegroom

*"The friend of the bridegroom, who stands and hears him,
rejoices greatly because of the bridegroom's voice. Therefore
this joy of mine is fulfilled." (John 3:29)*

In the popular wedding ceremonies of the East, it was the custom
for the friends of the bridegroom to parade the groom through the
city on horseback or by automobile, and the joyful pageant was usually accompanied by the sounds of strings and trumpets. Everyone's
face would light up with joy.

St. John the Baptist entered the world at this critical moment in
world history to be the first of those friends to lead the bridegroom
in the parade, and he did it with ecstatic shouts and cries. When
his task was completed, the bridegroom appeared to announce the
fullness of time and the start of the acceptable year. This appearance was the happiest day of John's mission, for when he heard the
bridegroom's voice, he said, "My joy is fulfilled." With the coming

of Christ came the revelation of the door, the way, and the bride, all at the same time. And the bride and bridegroom are now together in their wedding chamber, the Church. Joy has filled the entire household.

The Christian servant of the New Testament is not just the bridegroom's friend—that is, one who is happy to hear His voice, who leads Him in the parade up to the door of the wedding chamber, then takes his leave—but he is also the object of the bridegroom's own joy, for he is in the place of the bride and is a part of her. Every priest or servant also shares in the bridegroom's joy over His bride; he rejoices for the bridegroom and with the bridegroom.

Serving the bridegroom is total joy, total elation, and total delight, especially when the servants themselves are co-participants with the bride and bridegroom in the wedding. The bridegroom's servants are also the leaders of the marriage feast; and so there is absolutely no excuse for a hint of melancholy or gloom to be found in them, lest they offend the groom. And the bridegroom is always present in our midst in the Church: "Lo, I am with you always, *even* to the end of the age" (Matt. 28:20).

The bridegroom's task as overseer of His Church is eternal, mystical, and immutable: "You now have sorrow; but I will see you again and your heart will rejoice, and your joy no one will take from you" (John 16:22). Indeed, when Christ showed Himself to the disciples after His Resurrection, they were filled with a joy that itself became the essence and substance of the Gospel. For it was the joy of that revelation that inspired them to go out and spread the joyful news—that is, to preach Christ, the living and visible bridegroom.

St. Peter strives to reassure our doubting eyes of the truth when he says, "Though now you do not see *Him*, yet believing, you rejoice with joy inexpressible and full of glory" (1 Pet. 1:8). The people of the Old Testament waited for the joyful news—the message of hope and salvation—with much patience, and they repented upon hearing it. "How beautiful are the feet of those who preach the gospel of peace, who bring glad tidings of good things" (Rom. 10:15; Is. 52:7). The power in the priest's evangelism and the servant's teaching is directly drawn from their joy in the bridegroom. For rejoicing in God is the Gospel, and the Gospel is rejoicing in God.

2. Joy in the Repentance of Sinners

It is startling, even unsettling, to consider the close spiritual bond between saints and angels in heaven and repentant sinners on earth: "I say to you that likewise there will be more joy in heaven over one sinner who repents than over ninety-nine just persons who need no repentance" (Luke 15:7). This is a spiritual joy that surpasses the limits of our understanding. It is the one kind of joy that has been predestined before eternity, and it is the natural happiness that comes from a life of fellowship with Christ. How marvelous, how astonishing is Christ, who joined those in heaven with those on earth, who reconciled spirit and flesh, who demolished their enmity and united the two into one!

However, even more astounding is how a servant enters into this joy, participates and lives in it, and feeds on it: "My joy is *the joy* of you all" (2 Cor. 2:3). Is not the priest or servant the one responsible for steering sinners toward repentance, for opening to them the doors of paradise, for introducing them to the very joy of heaven? So it is a grave problem, one for which I find no easy solution, when I see a dejected priest carrying out his ministry with a glum face or when a depressed servant gives a joyless talk on salvation.

Is it right to give a sermon on the joys of heaven if the sermon does not make the listener joyful? Can the bride's family lead her in the procession to her groom while they are bowed down by grief? Can the Gospel take on another name or description? Is it not the "good news"? Is it not joyful and good for the sinful and righteous alike, for servants and the served alike? Is it not joyful for those in heaven too?

"And they overcame him by the blood of the Lamb and by the word of their testimony, and they did not love their lives to the death. Therefore rejoice, O heavens, and you who dwell in them!" (Rev. 12:11, 12)

3. Joy in the Power of God's Word

The essence of Christian service is usually assumed to be leading sinners to repentance. However, its truer and greater essence is to relay joy in Christ to the hearts of people. If a sinner does not find joy in Christ—joy that alone can make him richer than everything in this world—the abilities of the servant or his understanding of the ministry are proven to be gravely deficient.

One of the aims of the Christian servant should be to continually gain renewed strength through reading and contemplation. The sign that this strength has been gained is the appearance of a solid and lasting joy in the servant's heart as well as the discovery of God's voice in the Scripture he reads. The cheerful and joyful servant, who easily and perpetually quotes the words of Scripture, is a living and faithful picture of what the Gospel (i.e., "the good news") is.

4. Joy in the Growth of Others

> "He must increase, but I must decrease." (John 3:30)

The servant's principal work, or his central characteristic, is to give unceasingly, unwearyingly, generously, unconditionally, and without limit. The servant gives to the weak that they may become strong, and he gives to the strong that they may become steadfast. The servant gives to friend, stranger, and foe alike. He gives without favoritism or partiality. He gives of his possessions, experience, and spirit.

Now, if the source of the giving is genuinely divine, then we will inevitably see the servant's sincere joy at the increase and growth of others, even if it be at the cost of his own decrease. Christ Himself blesses this true and love-filled giving when it is done without any hope for compensation or repayment.

When a priest or servant "gives" cautiously and reluctantly for fear that people will devalue his knowledge, or for fear that others might supersede him in some way, he makes it impossible to find joy in his act of giving or in the growth of others. He is ultimately just a merchant of ideas rather than an authentic servant. "I will very gladly spend and be spent for your souls; though the more abundantly I love you, the less I am loved. But be that *as it may*" (2 Cor. 12:15, 16).

5. Joy at the Call to Serve Jesus Christ

When St. Paul makes the statement, "This *is* a faithful saying: If a man desires the position of a bishop, he desires a good work" (1 Tim. 3:1), he establishes that Christian service in and of itself is a good deed. Therefore, if we seek it on the basis that it is work, a series of deeds, this is good. But if we seek to join the service without our mind and conscience being focused on the idea that we must do good, then our desire is a poor, lifeless ambition.

The salient point in St. Paul's words is that Christian service (that is, the act of laboring in the Church) is in itself a very desirable thing. It is something to be sought after and loved with all the heart, because a Christian servant serves Jesus Himself. For we love Jesus, and our love for Him surpasses our natural limitations and transcends our natural minds. Our love for Him reaches to the very borders of death itself, and death can never separate us from His love. He rejoices in our love for Him and expects it of us. In this exchange of love, we are the true winners. Christ indicated that the vital sign of our sincere love for Him is our readiness to serve Him and to tend His sheep: "Do you love Me? . . . Tend My sheep" (John 21:16).

Any person called to serve Christ—whether because of his personal love for Christ or by the inspiration of God or others—must simply accept the burden of service as a consequence of his love. If he does so, God will stamp His seal on the authenticity of the calling and on the certainty that it will lead him to divine joy: "Enter into the joy of your lord" (Matt. 25:23).

If we focus on what is of real value in our service—the glory that accrues to Christ as a result of our words and deeds, and the liberation from the devil's slavery that it brings to people—we will immediately realize that the joy that springs from our service is not the joy of this present world. For the glory that is due Christ is better than the accolades of a thousand angels. "What then? Only *that* in every way, whether in pretense or in truth, Christ is preached; and in this I rejoice, yes, and will rejoice. For I know that this will turn out for my deliverance" (Phil 1:18, 19).

6. Joy in the Mystery of Suffering

Not everyone who suffers is able to taste the joy that is born of suffering. To many, suffering appears to be an incomprehensible thing. From the natural point of view, pain and joy are direct contradictions. But we affirm that the two are joined in a mysterious manner. Mystery always rises above nature. Here we are speaking about the mystery of joy that springs from the mystery of suffering.

The Christian servant and priest are, first and foremost, ministers of the mystery of Christ's suffering. No one can preach the mystery of Christ's suffering without himself being a partaker of that suffering: "God *is* faithful, by whom you were called into the fellowship of His Son, Jesus Christ our Lord" (1 Cor. 1:9). Our fellowship in the life of Christ is based on a fellowship in His pain, and the mystery of His pain is linked with the mystery of His joy: "Jesus . . . for the joy that was set before Him endured the cross, despising the shame" (Heb. 12:2). Any fellowship between two intimate people, such as a bride and groom, necessitates a reciprocal sharing in one another's sorrows and joys as well as a mutual revelation of the secrets in each other's hearts.

The Lord reveals the secret of His pain only to His especially beloved, to those who are intimate with Him. He does not communicate this mystery by knowledge, lectures, or books, but by granting them a share of His sufferings exactly proportionate to the joy and glory that await them: "For to you it has been granted on behalf of Christ, not only to believe in Him, but also to suffer for His sake" (Phil. 1:29). Can a bride really share in her groom's joy without also sharing in his pain? Can a person genuinely love his friend while avoiding a share in his sufferings?

The Lord grants us today a practical means of fellowship in the mystery of His suffering, for without that it is impossible to enter into the mystery of everlasting joy, a foretaste of which we are given even now. Any servant or minister who abides in true fellowship with Christ can never taste the Lord's joy without also tasting His pain; neither will he ever be given a portion of Christ's pain without also receiving a portion of His joy. If joy ever vanishes from a suffering heart, it is an indication that the Bridegroom is absent. For Christ's presence changes the "flavor" of suffering. The image of Him crowned with thorns and exhaling His last breath is enough to sweeten our pain with the joy that follows the Cross.

The priest or servant who has settled into a regular and heartfelt routine of prayer and has established an authentic and covenantal relationship with the Lord will no longer live for himself but will dedicate all the aspects of his life to participation in Christ's life. As Christ's suffering becomes his own, his own suffering becomes

Christ's; eventually, like St. Paul, he will "fill up in [his] flesh what is lacking in the afflictions of Christ" (Col. 1:24). As the servant progresses in maturity, so will he progress in the life of self-denial, until his entire existence moves from the realm of the flesh to the realm of the spirit.

Once the priest or servant reaches the point at which his suffering is continuously consecrated by Christ's suffering, he has reached the summit of this mystery of joy!

PART TWO

On the Education
of the Christian Servant

CHAPTER 10

The Making of a Servant of the Church

1. What Is a Servant of the Church?

A servant of the Church is not someone who has studied the ecclesiastical sciences and earned a degree in them, for the Spirit of the Church cannot be studied. Instead, it irrigates the soul: "We . . . have all been made to drink into one Spirit" (1 Cor. 12:13). The Church's Spirit is not contained in books, for a living and acting energy cannot be forced into a curriculum or a system of knowledge. The Spirit comes from Christ firstly, lastly, and always. The mind of Christ is His Spirit: "The words that I speak to you are spirit, and *they* are life" (John 6:63). It is true that His words often come through teachers and books, but they must also come through Christ Himself.

Therefore, a servant of the Church cannot be recommended by a mere written statement, for his recommendation must be the living testimony that emerges from within the Church. The sanctuary testifies to him because of his continual presence in it, because he enters in with a purified heart and body, with holy tears, and the redemptive blood of Christ. The altar and vessels testify to him and to his cleansed hands, which handle the sacred things with reverent care.

The choir testifies to him as an integral part of its harmony in worship. He has a consistent place allotted to him in the choir; his face shines with devotion for his fellow Christians; the priest rejoices to see him standing straight as a soldier and singing as exquisitely as a lark; the congregation recognizes him as a pillar in the church, moving about and lighting up the hearts of the worshippers with joy and goodwill; and the feasts and special occasions of the Church receive his wise and enthusiastic participation in their hymns, readings, rites, and splendor.

A servant of the Church cannot be commended simply for having many books or for acquiring much knowledge; rather, he is commended by the Spirit of Christ, who is charged and inflamed within him every day by the prayers and sacraments of the Church and by the voice of Christ in the Gospel. Again, the servant of the Church will not be commended for preaching from pulpits before first being commended for his presence among the ordinary ranks of supplicants, by his solemn ministrations at the altar, and by his engagement in the holy liturgy and his reception of the holy things. How can a servant communicate Christ to others without himself drawing upon Christ's Spirit? How can a person consider himself a servant of Christ without paying heed to the service of His house?

It makes little sense for a servant to seek commendation by studying the religious books of East or West and accumulating quotations from every random writer he comes across in any random language, if, at the same time, he is ignorant of his own Church's books, language, practices, and prayers. This type of servant will sometimes be deluded into thinking that his only rightful place in Church is the pulpit;[6] accordingly, he will spend all his time outside of church practicing for his performance at the pulpit, even calculating the quickest

---

6   In the Coptic Church, although a priest normally delivers the homily, a prominent layman is occasionally invited to serve as a substitute preacher for the day.

route to seizing it for himself. Such a person refuses to meekly enter church by the main door like everyone else; rather, he is like a thief who climbs up walls and enters through the side window.

A servant of the Church is not to be commended for preparing good lessons, nor for selecting the best verses, nor for his mode of delivery, nor for his perfect attendance record in church. What does commend him is the character of his life inside the Church, his love and zeal and solicitude for her, the satisfaction he finds in her history and saints, and the inner sense that he is a true member of her body. The question is, how is such a servant made? And what sort of proof certifies him as a true servant?

2. A Practical Method for Creating a Servant of the Church

If we seek a practical means to become filled with the life of the Church, we must realize that what we seek is far beyond anything the world can offer. To put it simply, we are entering into a mystery: the mystery of Christ and His Church. Before we can penetrate the mystery of Christian service, we must understand that Christianity is not a theory or philosophy, nor is it a rule of ethical conduct or a system of rites and practices. First and foremost, it is a new life, a life of regeneration, a life of simplicity, a life of love and humility. It has one goal: the union of Christ with His people. This union that binds us to Christ and to other Christians is what we call the Church.

Christian ministry, therefore, must necessarily find both its starting point and its final destination in the Church. In other words, the purpose and culmination of Christian service is to achieve the state in which servants and served alike become one in Christ in shared love, in shared trust, and in true humility. This unity must embrace absolutely everyone in the fold, from the greatest to the smallest member, until every barrier and dividing wall has been lifted. It is only through the fulfillment of this unity that knowledge and virtue truly flourish, spiritual gifts are bestowed, the Spirit finds rest in the Church, and Christ rejoices and lives among His people. In this way, the ministry and the Church prosper.

The mystery of service is hidden and diffused among the various prayers and liturgies of the Church, for the Church's eucharistic litanies and prayers constitute her very spirit. We may also say that they are the Church's lungs, by which the Holy Spirit breathes. Christ's blood passes through these lungs, oxygenating the eternal life of His people. All who participate in this breath of life are renewed and invigorated day by day. It is the duty of the servant and teacher of the Church to plumb the innermost depths of this fellowship of life, so that he may discover its wonders for himself and reveal its riches and blessings to others. He will be able to say to people, "Oh, taste and see that the LORD *is* good!" (Ps. 34:8). But if he has not seen and tasted the Lord's goodness, how can he proclaim it? Religious instruction in the Orthodox tradition has always been, before anything else, the teachings of its prayers and liturgy.

The best way to ensure the Church's successful teaching is to nourish her children by prayer and liturgy before trying to analyze and explain them. Taste must come before knowledge; experience must precede understanding. Experiential spirituality is the sole road to personal growth. Even if a child were to become the disciple of the most famous teachers and pedagogues of the Church, he will learn nothing unless the spiritual instruction is implanted in his will and conscience, rather than his mind. Thus, the prayers and liturgies of the Church are our best spiritual instructors, and nothing can compare to their ability to feed and nourish one's heart and mind.

If a servant has finished all the stages of childhood without having received the spirit of the Church, the opportunity for growth still remains, and the door stands wide open. For reception of the Spirit is not facilitated by one's age but by the amount of one's zeal and love.

Just the servant's participation in church services and his openness to the subtle movements of the Spirit are enough to clarify his vision of divine things and to deepen his understanding of religious knowledge, without excessive labor or forcing the mind. For the humility of mind and devotion of heart that descend on the soul during times of prayer are sufficient to raise the mind above its normal capacity, so much so that a person becomes astonished at the amount of change and progress he can achieve.

Do you see, then, how the mystery of humility and devotion that inspires a person during liturgy also causes the mystery of knowledge and clear vision to inspire him, which in turn leads him to a deeper understanding of God? Do not be surprised then, dear servant, when we state that the mystery of Christian service is contained in the mystery of the liturgy.

As we have said before, the ultimate goal of the Christian servant is not contemplation or theological aptitude, but rather the forming of a bond of love with Christ and other people. The servant's participation in the liturgy is his best opportunity to achieve a deep and lasting state of humility, one that is capable of shaking his being to its very foundations and knocking his pride down to the ground. This paves the way for an attitude of compunction and an openness to living in love and reconciliation with other people. Thus, through the liturgy the barriers to unity fall, and the servant enters more fully day by day into the great mystery of unity with others and with Christ. It is at this point that the service reaches its full measure of success, and the servant achieves his definitive goal.

But take heed! For the Divine Liturgy can be either a living or a dead thing. And what makes it alive or dead is precisely your heart and your faithfulness—that is, the integrity of your openness to God, as well as your repentance, humility, love, and acceptance of others.

3. The Ranks of Service

We have discussed the practical approach to creating a servant of the Church. Now, to ensure that the said servant will remain pious, carrying out his task adequately, he should be placed in a defined rank within the Church. This rank must correspond to his spiritual level, and it may increase as his spiritual maturity increases. The first rank is that of reader (*anagnostis*), then subdeacon, which means "deacon's helper," then deacon (which literally means "servant").

However, a truth that we must clearly understand and safeguard to the best of our ability is that the Church does not recognize any type of service that has broken from her official ranks. This is why religious instruction in the Church today has wandered so far from its original path. If things continue thus, every servant will have his own personal rank custom-tailored to his particular circumstances and aims. The most dangerous thing is to freely nominate and ordain people to the ranks of service before they have received a sound and thorough training in ecclesiastical service.

Preparatory courses for servants of the Church should receive the blessing and instruction of the clergy, of brethren specialized in the knowledge of the Church and her language, of chanters and psalmists, of servants devoted to the Church's mission in the world, and of spiritual fathers. The curriculum should be divided into several different levels corresponding to the respective ranks of service in the Church, from reader to deacon. In addition, a servant should not be advanced from one rank to the next without formal testing, letters of recommendation, and a formal commitment by the candidate to the service of the rank in question. The person advancing the candidate must inscribe his name in the official records of the Church, and he must furnish the candidate with a certificate that clearly defines the obligations of the rank to which he has been committed.

With this official structure in place, the head or leader of the servants will be responsible before God and the bishop for the oversight of the other servants (deacons), their helpers (subdeacons), the youth leaders, religious instruction in general, and the testing of those eligible for advancement. In the tradition of the Coptic Church, every rank of deacon is answerable to the archdeacon, while the archdeacon is directly answerable to the bishop. Thus, we do not truly need to create new rules or revise the received system; what we do need is respect for church laws and an effort to implement them. We must emphasize over and over again that the inherent value of the Church's organization will be manifested only when its stewards take it seriously and enforce it faithfully, for it is intended to function as a gateway to eternal life.

CHAPTER II

The Psychological Health of the Servant

I

The greatest obstacle that stands in the way of the growth and improvement of Christian service (as intended by the Bible and the Fathers) is the feeble state of most servants' spiritual lives. And the chief cause of the weak spiritual state of today's servants is their enfeebled psychological state; thus, it is necessary to strengthen a servant's psychological state and personality before we attempt to rectify his spiritual life.

The Holy Fathers themselves insisted that only the psychologically sound and balanced self is capable of becoming spiritual, for the balanced mind alone can perceive divine truth. The mind that is weighed down by faults, weaknesses, and defects, in contrast, cannot serve as a calm resting place for the Holy Spirit and thus cannot clearly see divine light. However, when we speak of psychological "faults, weaknesses, and defects," we are not referring to common sins (which also corrode the human psyche and prevent its reception of divine light), such as lying, hypocrisy, greed, ambition, bribery, uncleanness, pride, self-righteousness, self-admiration, the pursuit of

+ III +

praise, and the rest of the sins that ensnare servants and laypeople alike. These we may leave to one side for the present, for they may be considered "particular" sins that can be treated by methods outside the arena of official church service.

We need to distinguish between such common sins and the psychological defects that beset Christian servants in particular. The difference is as great as the difference between an isolated illness that afflicts the eye (like conjunctivitis) and total blindness. Conjunctivitis is particular and acute, whereas blindness is general and chronic. And if our desire is to help the service in general, we must focus our efforts on the chronic ailments first. What exactly are those flaws, weaknesses, or psychological defects that affect the psychological state of Christian servants, stop the increase of their spiritual stature, and prevent the light from reaching them?

We will limit our discussion to three psychological flaws that afflict the current generation of servants: a "follower mentality," ideological or emotional partisanship, and bad habits arising from improper upbringing.

1. A Follower Mentality

Christian servants these days have a tendency to follow blindly any new teaching, personality, or idea that strikes their fancy. This phenomenon is most evident in the new generation of servants, and it was nearly absent from the preceding generations. The preceding generation knew how to wisely discern between personalities, and we must state with full admiration how noble, reliable, fruitful, and authoritative many of the older servants were. The majority of them were made into honorable bishops, reverend priests, monks, learned scholars of the Church, or they were otherwise consecrated to the Church's ministry. However, the current generation of servants is severely lacking in the personal qualities needed for such roles, in large part because their autonomous spirit has been exchanged for a follower mentality. Several ingredients have combined to produce such an unsavory "stew."

The first ingredient is the lack of proper leadership in the preparation of young people for service. We have said that training youth for service does not mean preaching at them or making them attend liturgies or imposing curricula on them for the duration of one or two years. Rather, training young servants means entering into a life of fellowship with them. The leader must test their capabilities, rectify their flaws, straighten their thinking, and sharpen their spiritual awareness. In short, he must lay the foundations of their spiritual character. He is to oversee the development of the fine details of their personalities, so that they may in the end be fit for their particular roles in the ministry.

The second ingredient is the tendency of certain leaders to build themselves up as the one and only door to true knowledge. The servants are forced to concern themselves more with the nature and traits of their teacher's personality than with the teaching itself. Declaring allegiance to the leader's image becomes a requirement to receive his teaching. Gradually, the service transforms into a competition that involves building a loyal group of followers and handing out "favors" to stay "in the lead." The free and autonomous spirit of the servants is thus replaced by a subservient clinging to the personality of the teacher.

The third ingredient is the way children have been raised at home in the past few decades, effectively erasing their strength of character.[7] Child rearing has virtually taken the form of a dictatorship, where fathers have held their ideas to be a sort of dogma and

---

7   This paragraph refers to conditions in Egypt at the time the book was written. In America, conditions are essentially opposite to this description, which carries its own problems.

employed methods of discipline that were aimed to stamp their children's character with a particular religious and behavioral mold that was agreeable to the father's conceptions but irrelevant to the children's abilities. Thus the parents of the current generation have colluded in the demolition of their children's character from childhood.

The fourth ingredient is the dwindling of the practice of confession and spiritual guidance, which is due in large part to the dereliction of confessors and spiritual fathers. Many spiritual fathers have assumed their position of spiritual authority before achieving the spiritual caliber needed for shouldering such a serious responsibility. Church tradition used to dictate that a priest could not become a father confessor before the age of fifty. It was assumed that only then would the marks of wisdom, spiritual insight, and the penetrating vision needed to understand and heal souls begin to manifest themselves in his life and actions. At that point, the bishop would read a special prayer over him and grant him the right to hear confessions. He would then be known as an "elder" in the Church and be regarded with great esteem by the whole congregation.

But what happens today is that any young man who is ordained to the priesthood is automatically considered a father confessor. You may even find a young person barely out of his adolescence entering a monastery with the sincere intent to begin a life of repentance and never again to return to the world, but after one or two years, without anyone realizing it, he finds his way back into the world and begins hearing confessions! The question that screams out at us is this: How can a spiritual guide or father confessor edify people's lives when he himself suffers from acute personal problems? How can such a person guide others when he has not attained the spiritual level that qualifies him for the formidable task of saving souls?

As for servants, oftentimes these days they use the practice of confession and spiritual guidance as a tacit means to complete the process of character-stripping that began at home. Confession is used as an excuse for servants to justify their actions. Hence the familiar formula, "My father confessor blessed me to . . . ," which is conveniently used to absolve a servant of all personal responsibility. Too often spiritual fathers insist on a total and blind obedience. This imperceptibly erases the servant's personality, not only sparing him the burden of responsibility for his personal actions but even deluding him into considering it virtuous! Spiritual guides themselves encourage young servants to forfeit their personalities in the interest of following and admiring the personalities of their superiors instead.

2. Ideological and Emotional Partisanship

This psychological flaw is the direct result of having a follower's mentality, because being a follower of a certain person naturally begets an unreasonable and fanatical bias toward him. It is unfortunate to observe that almost all servants of the Church have contracted this disease. When a servant is a follower, he often becomes a partisan. This habit of partisanship in turn makes him fanatical. This process ends in the eradication of his own personality. When a person's own personality is eradicated, he is compelled to seek refuge in another's personality and to cling to it tenaciously. For he "finds himself" only in the presence of that other personality, and in its absence, it is as if he doesn't exist.

The follower's partisanship or bias toward his idol can be either ideological or emotional, depending on his state of mind and emotions. If the follower has a sound mind, then the nature of his bias will be emotional. If he has stable emotions, on the other hand, then his bias will be ideological. Naturally, if he is both intellectually and emotionally sound, he won't be a partisan at all, for he won't be a follower to begin with.

The presence of this sort of partisanship and personal bias in Christian service is extremely damaging to the spirit of Christianity itself, for it hinders the servants from rising to a living vision of Christ. Christ's own face is hidden behind the veil of renowned "personalities." St. Paul remarks several times in his epistles (1 Cor. 1:10–17; 1 Cor. 3:1–4) that any bias toward persons and names is a sure sign of a failing spiritual state among believers as well as a great blight upon church life and worship.

3. Bad Habits Arising from Incorrect Upbringing

Another characteristic that seems preponderant among the current generation is the average servant's inability to extricate himself from the incorrect habits of his own family. He enters the field of service with his mind and behavior already tarnished by certain defects for which he cannot be entirely blamed, but which nevertheless handicap his spiritual life, rendering him unfit for the service. Several bad habits have especially pernicious effects:

- Some families have a habit of poor treatment of servants who visit the home. They effectively estimate them as being below the normal standard of regular people. Such families refuse visiting servants the most basic hospitalities by offering them the worst food available; by totally disregarding their feelings, their health, and their comfort; and by taking no pains to offer them a kind welcome. Rather, their aim is to deny them every right due to a normal guest and to deny them any recompense for their efforts. They use every wily and twisted means to rid the home of their presence. We mention this fault first because it is enough to bring any servant's enthusiasm down to the dirt.
- Pride in his family's bloodline, name, wealth, title, or reputation naturally infects the servant with a vaunting sense of superiority and excessive self-admiration. It is a character defect that makes

the servant incompatible with the homes and people he serves. Even if he outwardly displays a zeal for serving the young and the poor, inwardly he remains detached and unsympathetic toward them. He is simply not able to stoop sincerely and openly to their level. His is a condescending service, one not remarkable for any real sacrifice or charity. This obliterates the true spirit of service and destroys hope for any spiritual growth. As long as the servant remains pleased with his own talents and satisfied with himself thanks to the apparent success of his activity, his service will remain in a state of spiritual poverty.

+ Some families have a tendency toward being isolated and focused on only their own needs. Such families attempt to live in complete isolation from other branches of their own extended family because of their self-proclaimed exceptionalism. This isolationist spirit will naturally breed a type of personal exceptionalism in the servant. If a servant imbibes this spirit early in life and fails to banish it in time, his main focus in the ministry will be to isolate and insulate his unique service from all the other ministries in the Church. He may use certain subtle and psychological means (even threats) with the friends and youth who follow him to isolate them from the rest, and even to pit them against other people as a way of cementing their loyalty. The tragic result of this game-playing is the youth's own absorption of the servant's separatist spirit and the loss of his ability to love and mingle and unite with other youth. Hence, spiritual unity—the one great aim of Christian service, the most essential characteristic of the Church, and the ultimate desire of Christ on the Cross—is destroyed.

+ Some parents have a controlling or domineering spirit. Even if the damaging effects of this psychological defect are not as far-reaching as the previous three, it is still present in a large number of today's servants. Some fathers in Orthodox homes rule their families in a high-handed manner, and their obsession with control drives them to deny their children the most basic rights and freedoms they deserve, even after their children have entered adulthood. These children (who are the current generation of servants) have no choice but to cower before the aggressive iron grip of their fathers. Many conflicts in modern families are a result of this authoritarianism, for the children have inherited this imperious spirit. It has become implanted in their character, like a hereditary part of their nature. Now, when one of these children, who were made a sacrifice to their parents' tyranny, becomes a servant of the Church, his stifled personality immediately gives vent through his service, and the portentous signs of the same despotism begin to be revealed in him. However, it disguises itself under the cloak of a pious and fatherly "concern for others." It justifies its imperious character by pleading its "zeal" for the service, and it justifies its domineering hold over the children by pleading its "anxiety" for their well-being and their future. And in order to guarantee the children's continued submission to himself, the servant will speak to them at length about the virtue of obedience, the necessity of obedience, and the benefits of obedience—the same type of rhetoric that was used with him when he was young.

The unfortunate consequence of all this is the proliferation of this character defect, or we should say character disaster, which was once isolated within the limits of a small family, but has now spread like an epidemic and has inflicted its damaging effects on the personalities of a whole generation of youth. It has threatened to forestall their spiritual growth and to steal from them that evangelical liberty which is one of the most prized gifts Christ has given to the Church.

But we may here end this sad description of the psychological problems that have beset the current generation of church servants and razed their spiritual status. As for the remedies to these problems, we will pursue that discussion in later chapters—leaving for now each servant to silently contemplate these issues within himself.

2

In the previous sections, we spoke about the problems that afflict servants of the Church and the ministry in general. In this section, we will focus on certain positive approaches we can take to overcome these shortcomings. For when the servants find strength, the entire ministry is strengthened. So, what are the strengths of a successful servant of the Church?

First, a strong servant has a clearly defined goal for his ministry, one that he firmly believes in, diligently pursues, and loves, and in which he finds his joy. Second, he has a spiritual role model who encourages him, helps guide his thoughts, reignites his enthusiasm when it cools, and urges him to persevere in his work. Third, he has an active and steadfast will that single-mindedly strives for his goal. Fourth, he labors with the full energy of his mind and body to realize his objectives. In this, he finds his joy. Let us take each of these in turn.

1. The Servant's Goal

We have placed one's goal in life as the most important factor that determines a servant's success, for it gathers and focuses the various aspects of a servant's personality, no matter how undetermined or undeveloped it may still be. In other words, the appearance of a definitive goal in a person's life induces his character to begin forming itself around it; the will, the emotions, and the role models that guide a person's life are all determined by it. Conversely, when a person loses track of his goal in life, his will weakens, his emotions run astray, and the models to which he once looked vanish from his mind. The end result is the deterioration and dissolution of his character.

Indeed, it is this goal that is primarily responsible for either the growth or the dissolution of one's character. And whether one's personality is sound or unstable plays an enormous role in the health of that person's spiritual life. A sound personality that possesses clear goals, a steady will, steady emotions, and diligent action will have self-control; he will not fall prey to the demands of his biological drives or become captive to capricious and tyrannical impulses. Conversely, the unstable personality that is guided by neither right goals nor a steady will is doomed to become the plaything of bodily drives, turbulent emotions, and sudden impulses.

For these reasons, here is the best advice that can be given to a servant who complains about his psychological state and who earnestly desires a sound, steady, and self-controlled character: he must clarify what his goal is, and he must always place that goal before his eyes. The ministry in and of itself should never be the goal, for the goal ought to be higher than the ministry.

What, then, is the ultimate goal of Christian service?

If a person's service involves personal gain of any kind, then the goals that motivate the service cannot be considered spiritual at all. One's service must be totally free of personal gain; love and sacrifice should be its only motives. Therefore, we must constantly test the motives that inspire us to serve, so that personal gain is shunned and love and sacrifice are exalted. Emotions and selfish drives must never control our ministry, but rather love for God first and an impartial love for people second.

If a servant wishes to maintain an upright character in his serving, he must always have before his eyes a clear and consistent goal. And there can be no clearer goal than to offer love in the form of sacrifice and to love God until the servant has such a finely tuned sense of what is right that he can detect even the slightest leaning of his motives toward the ego.

The slightest bit of self-gain is enough to completely distort one's aim in service. It can deform the service itself into a sort of plague that consumes the servant's personality, making self-love the ultimate aim of his efforts and aspirations. The "sacrifices" he makes for service are then no longer sacrifices, but rather a kind of business or trade, for inasmuch as he gives, he expects to receive in return. The more he receives, the more he wants to "sacrifice." Thus, the service becomes a business with his depraved self at the center. This proves the vital need for a spiritual guide who can model genuine love and sacrifice and who can correct the servant's errors from their very inception.

2. The Spiritual Role Model

There are many fine examples of sacrifice in the history of the Church. One may look at the Apostle Paul, who suffered the loss of everything he had and counted it as rubbish for the sake of Christ and His ministry. One may desire to be like Stephen, who surrendered his body to stoning as the price for speaking the truth and for his witness to Christ. Or one may want to be like Athanasius, who stood against the world until his last breath to safeguard the faith entrusted to him. The examples we could cite are almost endless, and such stories are indeed effective in igniting our enthusiasm and empowering our thoughts and actions to pursue our service diligently.

At the same time, such examples may conceivably be used to bolster one's ego. We should fear lest a servant's eyes be shifted away from the real sacrifice of these saints and martyrs and be focused instead on their fame and reputation. When this happens, Christian service becomes a means of displaying one's abilities for the sake of winning the same fame and reputation as these saints of old. St. Paul therefore says, "Imitate me, just as I also *imitate* Christ" (1 Cor. 11:1), which means, "If you want to be like me, first see how I was like Christ."

We have no excuse for neglecting our search for a spiritual role model. Once found, we will never be able to use him as an excuse to fulfill our personal interests; in fact, he will be a model for the death of our interests. And what better model for such things than Jesus Christ? He is the only one who can live in us and put our selfish interests totally to death. "It is no longer I who live, but Christ lives in me" (Gal. 2:20). It is good when Christ lives in a servant's being—in his mind, his heart, his spirit, and his members. It is good when Christ is a spiritual role model for his service, sacrifice, and unconditional love.

Consider Christ's life. See Him going about doing good, with the crowds pressing about to kiss His hands and feet and robe, being immersed in acts of mercy, driven solely by love, focused not on Himself, but on the Cross prepared for Him at the road's end, for it is the true crown of His ministry.

See Him caught up in those loving and compassionate dialogues held with the disciples, with Judas also in their midst. See Him speaking to Judas with the same love and compassion, not dwelling on the imminent betrayal, the treacherous kiss, or the thirty pieces of silver.

See Him passing quickly through the crowds who stood amazed at His words and deeds, shunning those hands stretched forth to seize and make Him king, for He did not come to sit in the lofty seats of kings but to submit to death.

See Him insulted and forsaken, beaten and stripped naked, carrying His cross to the place of crucifixion, all in order to fulfill the loving will of the Father who sent Him.

We cannot have a greater model of love, sacrifice, and obedience to God in ministry than this. He is the only role model who can expel all egotistical motives and crooked ambitions from our souls. No other model is more worthy of our love; no other can provide such impetus for our will or achieve such a beneficent dominion over our mind. How indelible on the heart of man is the image of His head crowned with thorns! No other example is so able to inflame the heart with zeal, to the point that love and sacrifice no longer have limits and the hardest services become light and desirable, even though they be contrary to our very nature, though they carry in them an invitation to die.

If we deem the idea of a role model to be necessary for any person looking to achieve a noble cause, then Christ is the most necessary role model of all. This is especially true if a servant wants to keep his enthusiasm alive and his motives pure. Conversely, if the absence of a role model means the cooling and quenching of a person's zeal, then the absence of Christ from a servant's life means the loosening of the will from the pursuit of its holy cause. In such cases, circumstances and moods step in to control the will and direct one's actions.

Therefore, the union of the highest goal in service, which is sacrifice, to Jesus Christ, who is the highest role model, can be considered the cornerstone of Christian service and the surest guarantee of the growth and edification of the servant.

3. A Diligent Will

On the one hand, the existence of the will to serve is tied to one's goal; on the other hand, the will's diligence is molded by the influence of the spiritual role model in the servant's heart. If the goal (sacrificial love) is near and dear to the heart, and if the role model (Christ Jesus) is likewise near and dear to the heart, then the servant will possess a will that is constantly eager, fervent, and active. However, if the servant ever finds his will weary or slacking, it's an indication that he needs to review his goals and role models. A weak will points to the fact that the servant must have lost sight of his inspiration—Christ—or his goal—love of sacrifice.

It is a commonly known truth that the emotions follow the lead of the will and unite with it. The will takes the role of the mother, and the emotions are her children. Just as a strong and responsible mother commands authority over her children, so does a strong and active will bring the emotions under its authority and employ them for spiritual work. But a weak will becomes thwarted by the emotions, which steer a person according to their own whims. The strength that we feed into our will earns for us dominion over our emotions and enables us to direct them to fulfill our goal (to sacrifice for love) for the glory of our role model (Christ), for whom we live.

Another commonly known truth is that one's will controls the direction not only of one's service but also of one's ordinary life. When we nourish our will, our character is strengthened, which in turn enables us better to face the challenges of life and of ministry in particular. However, bitter experiences, raw emotions, and selfish impulses can fight against the will and degrade man; collectively, these are sometimes referred to by scientists as a "repression complex." Such a complex exists secretly beneath the will and damages it to the point of harming the person's entire being. The only way to extirpate the complex and strengthen the will is by work—wholesome spiritual work that is guided by a spiritual father.

4. Spiritual Work

Of all the different means for man to build his character and empower his will, nothing compares to spiritual work. Work in general is extremely edifying, especially work that involves other people. The work must demand motion and energy, and it should be under the direction of a spiritual father or some other trustworthy supervisor. The most useful work of all is visiting others and doing them acts of kindness; this is, in fact, the greatest service that can be done for the servant's own sake as well. A servant who teaches others, not for the love of teaching but for the love of sacrifice; who visits others, not from a sense of being a dignified guest, but for the sake of entering into the circumstances of their existence; who shows mercy to the weak, the sick, and the poor, not from a sense of obligation, but from a sense of spiritual love that he imbibed from his role model— such a spiritual worker will daily strengthen his character, fortify his will, and dissolve the complexes in his mind. This is especially true if his spiritual father possesses a keen vision and is able to direct the details of the work and track its progress.

Finally, the day-to-day spiritual work that a servant performs throughout his whole life is a sufficient measure of the validity of the goal and purpose he has placed before himself. It is the measure of the efficacy of the spiritual role model whom he has chosen for himself. And it is the measure of the strength of his will to command his emotions and impulses.

The servant's level of commitment to his work reveals how profound his goal—sacrificial love—truly is.

The amount of fire and zeal in the servant's attitude toward service reveals how attached he is to his spiritual role model—Christ.

The amount of energy, persistence, and patience he shows in his service reveals how thoroughly he has dominated his will.

The amount of progress the servant makes in character growth and spiritual edification reveals how serious and important the ministry is to him.

Thus, the servant can see through his service a complete picture of his true spiritual and personal state.

As much as the service uncovers the psychological and personal weaknesses of the servant, so much also does the service itself become the healer and remedy for the servant's character. Thus, the psychological edification of the servant is accomplished only through service itself.

CHAPTER 12

The Spiritual Education of the Servant

INTRODUCTION

In this section, we will not discuss how a servant improves his spiritual life in general. Rather, we will focus specifically on the ways to enhance his spiritual credentials for serving the younger generation. Consequently, the assumption is that we are dealing with a group of servants who already have the necessary personal and mental qualities for ministry, and we will build upon those qualities to further refine their service. The question then is, what are the fundamental methods we must employ for the instructional and pastoral care of these servants?

We must remind ourselves, first of all, that the concept of "Christian spirituality" as understood in the Orthodox tradition is not something that can be achieved by merely studying the Bible or other religious books. Orthodox Christian spirituality is an experience that is handed down from one generation to the next.

This inheritance comprises the following:

- Ascetical life: prayer, fasting, and faithful, consistent participation in sacramental worship
- Doctrinal training: informing the believer of the tenets of faith and implanting belief so securely in the heart that it cannot be shaken by doubt or trouble
- Christian conduct: what should or should not be said and done, so that the conscience is groomed and trained in the fundamental values of the Orthodox Church
- The life in Christ: nurturing the essential love that brings a servant closer to God and increases his zeal, light, and discernment.

The reader should take note of the proper order of these traits. Ascetic practice comes at the very beginning of spiritual growth. We do not here refer to the asceticism of monks and archimandrites, but rather to spiritual work in general, such as prayer, fasting, and communal worship, all of which form the beginning stage of religious life. For spiritual life to be balanced and constant, it must be stabilized by correct Orthodox doctrine. Hence, doctrinal instruction constitutes a necessary corollary to ascetical life as its mainstay and bulwark against error. Next, since the Christian servant makes so many contacts with other people, his disposition and manner of behavior toward them is an important component of his work. Therefore, fitting speech and activity must be as a second nature. Finally, since spiritual service is not at heart about book learning, but in essence is the overflowing of one's soul, one must be constantly filled to the brim, so to speak, and so the servant's personal life must be filled with fresh spiritual experiences.

The ultimate aim that unifies all four factors to help spiritually edify the servant is the servant's perfect and complete personhood in Christ.

I

ASCETICAL LIFE

A Christian by definition should be an ascetical person who loves to pray and who finds joy in fasting and worship. A Christian servant is someone who strives to achieve perfection in this definition of Christianity. Therefore, his greatest desire is to make the commands of the Lord Jesus his rule of life—so much so that Christ's desires become his own.

1. Prayer

To the Christian servant, prayer is an ascetical work that is not a mere obligation or duty but the servant's daily sustenance. It is indeed the greatest ascetical work, through which the servant can channel the full capacity of his spiritual energy. Through prayer, God creates a new heart in him. Through prayer, the human heart is balanced and steadied. Through prayer, God finds a resting place in the heart, and then the heart finds its solace and peace in God. Ascetical prayer in the Orthodox tradition means prayer guided by fasts and the communal worship of the Church.

Ascetical prayer is also a creative act. It ceaselessly creates capabilities and powers that do not naturally stem from a person's character, which the person never even imagined he would one day possess.

The pinnacle of ascetical prayer is an intimate relationship with God through the mediation of the Holy Spirit. Here a servant finds the fulfillment of all his hopes and dreams. Then he is led by the Spirit of God so that his every work prospers.

Just as everyday prayer inspires the ordinary person with hope in times of trouble, so also ascetical prayer (that is, prayer fortified by fasting and communal worship) expands the nature, the mind, and the activity of the Christian servant to the point that they are united with God and flow from Him in a most remarkable way. Suffice it to say that prayer is the ultimate mystical source of man's spiritual strength, which is why it is the cornerstone of the servant's spiritual edification.

This is not the place to discuss the rules and principles of ascetical prayer, but we can at least note the profound importance of keeping the simple canonical rule of daily prayer. That rule calls for a person to pray three times in a twenty-four–hour period: once in the morning upon waking, once in the evening before sleep, and once at the "midnight hour," which means immediately before sunrise. Any prayer that exceeds this rule can be considered a gift of God's grace and favor.

True prayer will be characterized by intense supplication, repentance, prostrations, and an open Bible, so that the prayer can be enhanced by reading and be encouraged by God's promises. Psalms should be spoken with the heart and not merely with the lips. Prayer should widen the field for the soul's self-expression. The Christian servant must strive diligently to spend his days in prayer and his nights in praise.

2. Fasting

For the servant, fasting serves as a source of strength to face every sort of struggle. Fasting refines prayer, cleanses the heart of impurities, guards the soul from delusions, protects the mind from stress and restlessness, and controls and teaches the tongue to behave properly. Fasting is a spiritual weapon that effectively improves man's nature and trains his senses. Those who have agreed to take up this weapon for the sake of self-mastery have had their brows stamped with the insignia of God's regiment.

The fasting servant passes over the snares of the devil—offenses, attacks, and difficulties—with the ease of someone with wings.

Moreover, fasting qualifies a person for entrance into, and the contemplation of, the Spirit's mysteries, and Christ's sunlight will dawn upon him. When this happens, spiritual knowledge begins to grow within, as well as discernment and wise conduct, which are the chief gifts of the spiritual man.

This is not the place to discuss levels and methods of fasting, but we can at least say that it is necessary for the Christian servant to adhere to the practice and timing of the Church's fasts and never to shirk them as unwanted burdens. Fasting is a difficult but heavenly work that gives strong spiritual power. The more the servant fasts, the more robust his soul grows. If prayer is the foundation of spiritual edification, then fasting is the strength to bear the hardships involved in spiritual growth. In addition, a servant is in need of personal fasts assigned to him by his spiritual father to test his mettle.

3. Communal Worship

A Christian servant attends public prayer not as a mere spectator, but as a real participant. The deacon is a liturgical servant of the church, and a deacon is responsible for the proper and orderly execution of communal worship. He does not oversee prayers for himself alone but for the benefit of others. For a servant, communal worship is both self-fulfillment and self-sacrifice. He takes for himself and gives away. It is an immensely beneficial ascetical work that edifies the servant's soul and teaches him that he must give as much as he receives, he must be poured out as much as he is filled, and he must comfort others as much as he is himself comforted.

The Christian servant also participates in public worship by offering himself as a living example to others of the reverence and solemnity required in any person who approaches God. In the most sacred moments of communal worship, Christian teaching reaches its pinnacle. Orthodox doctrine reveals itself as most true when the servant and the served, the teacher and the pupil, all together ascend to an equal level of spiritual fulfillment. This spiritual edification comes directly from God. Although it may seem that the teacher is building up his pupil, in reality God is building them both up. Everyone is built with the same materials, and God builds them up into a single spiritual temple.

For a servant to enter fully into the seasons and worship of the Church is his greatest goal, both for himself and for his ministry. This is especially true if his private prayers complement the church's worship, for his whole life will shine forth as an illustrious example of spirituality for his pupils and disciples, who will glorify God through him. Finally, a servant should learn the essentials of psalmody and liturgical practice from a chanter or a deacon.

4. Contentment and Simple Living

To the Christian, any loss suffered for the faith's sake is profit and gain. How much more so for the Christian servant! A true servant even seeks the loss of his own will so that he might gain more. He freely forgoes personal leisure and passes up opportunities to make extra money at work in order to spend more time in the service. He perseveres in doing good so that he might produce a "profit" in other people's souls.

The world loses its enchantment in the eyes of a Christian servant, and it fails to prove itself as a place full of desirable goods. For his prayers, his fasts, and his worship give him spiritual eyes that accurately perceive the true value of things. When the world makes an offer of its advantages and glories to him, he finds little worth in them, for the treasures of his heart are stored up in heaven. He is satisfied with only the things of the world that are necessary for life. His heart's joy is not found in fine antiques or designer clothes or trinkets or any other worldly pleasures. His joy is in the sufficiency of the Spirit.

Money is an enchanting master that deludes the world and oppresses it by monstrous demands. But this master has no authority over the servant's heart; he knows it for a fraud. It is a mere underling that comes to serve its purpose and leaves, and the servant does not request of it anything more than what necessity calls for. When it increases, it is the Spirit's signal that the ministry must be increased, and when it is scarce, increased grace more than compensates for its lack.

Moreover, the novice servant must tithe faithfully; if grace works in his heart, no person or thing can ever convince him that he has given enough. He does not cease from giving as long as he has something to give. He continues to give until he reaches his very last resource; in fact, he does not rest until he has given his whole self. So, if "the love of money is the root of all kinds of evil, to make people stray from the faith in their greediness and pierce themselves through with many sorrows" (1 Tim. 6:10), then by the faithful stewardship of money, a Christian servant finds a clear opportunity for coming closer to God, for delving deeper in faith, and for depending more fully on grace. Paper bills and coins can become the material for real spiritual exercises that aid him on the road to the Kingdom.

In a similar vein, the amusements and pastimes of the world have become a pressing psychological need for modern man, and a person may exhaust most of his income in pursuing such activities. However, if a servant so much as looks at such things as the main source of mental diversion and spiritual comfort, they will instead trigger acute psychological anxiety. They will waste his time, deplete his health, dwindle his money, spoil his taste for prayer and spiritual activities, and weaken his resolve for repentance. A servant's consolation is his prayer; his amusement is the devoted reading of spiritual literature; his rest is confession; and his greatest happiness is the daily harvest of souls that occurs through his ministry.

Likewise, the craving for fame and a good reputation—something that has enslaved so many souls, compelled them to waste so much money and time, and forced them to grovel and lick the dust of the ground—is, in the eyes of the Christian servant, nothing but a trap and a delusion. To succumb to this enemy is to suffer a hard fall from which it is very difficult to rise. The soul that desires fame is like a ship carrying extremely bulky cargo, weighed down by its burden and sailing through such perilous and rocky waters that it is in imminent danger of sinking. Therefore, the wary soul spurns this craving with all its might, treading with great care to avoid its pitfalls. The shrewd servant will daily throw off such damaged and valueless goods from the ship of his soul. Thus he will become an accomplished spiritual merchant.

We come next to the passions and sexual impulses, which are the driving force behind the majority of people's greed, ambition, and selfishness in the modern world. Moreover, the passions are the secret source of modern man's frenzied activity as well as the hidden reason behind most of the conflicts that occur between families and nations. But to the Christian servant, these natural drives are turned into a type of incense offered at the altar of divine love. They are a radiant energy that emanates from the self. This energy does not denigrate the body by squandering its members' vitality on unworthy pleasures, but sublimates the body to the dignity of the spirit. The body thus turns into a spiritual flame that renovates the mind and illumines the path to eternal life.

The Christian servant can be compared to a tireless trader who never ceases bartering, exchanging every fleshly item that comes into his possession for a spiritual item. For example, the natural passions, which are generally regarded as stronger than any other emotive force, compelling him to fornication, are a type of "raw goods" that the spiritual servant can take hold of and convert into the spiritual "goods" of love, to further his relationship with God and his fellow man. He becomes a tireless lover who never quits until he has caught every other soul in the net of love that first caught him. "I have betrothed you to one husband, that I may present *you as* a chaste virgin to Christ" (2 Cor. 11:2).

Nevertheless, since the bodily passions are naturally implanted in the members of the body, and since the mind naturally directs a person's attention to the urgings of the body, it is imperative for the spiritual servant to toil by ascetic practice to redirect these natural urges toward something supernatural. Though he begins this struggle against the flesh with a negative mindset, in the end, his result will be positive. The servant's love will have been stripped of all sensuality and egotism, and he will lead other souls to the bosom of Christ. "I have betrothed you to one husband."

When the servant of Christ is thus freed from the control of the passionate emotions that make him captive to flesh and blood, and instead lives in the liberty of the Spirit that is fed and nourished by divine love, he becomes a skilled fisher of men. He will be a faithful keeper of Christ's net, ably throwing it over the lot of men, gently pulling it in, and emptying it directly into the bosom of Christ. But the servant who does not liberate himself from the passions of the flesh fishes for himself and not for Christ, and thus fritters away his gain.

Thus, considering the servant's role as a fisher of men, his ascetical exercises for the sake of dominance over the sexual passions are of primary importance. The fleshly impulses and emotions threaten to blemish the service with a fleshly stain, even to almost making it a form of sin. This will happen if the servant fails to be kindled by the flaming love of Christ, which alone is capable of burning up the ropes that bind him, for the fleshly lusts must lose their tyrannical hold before the body can live at peace and the soul can reflect the light of Christ's purity. There is no other way to acquire Christ's flame except by gradual and stepwise progress in ascetical practices and by resisting the desire for power, money, amusements, and distinction.

✠ ✠ ✠

To conclude our discussion of ascetical work, it is useful to summarize the stepwise progress of spiritual edification. The Christian servant cannot resist the assaults of the sexual drives without attending to his prayers. Prayer loses its power in the absence of fasting. If fasting is to confer strength, it must be accompanied by grace. Grace is not received without consistent participation in the worship and sacraments of the Church. Contentment will be acquired once the flesh is disarmed of the weapons it uses to war against the spirit. Finally, once the flesh is disarmed, the spirit will be immediately outfitted with the armor of God, with which it may tear down the ramparts of the enemy: "For the weapons of our warfare *are* not carnal but mighty in God for pulling down strongholds" (2 Cor. 10:4).

2

CHRISTIAN DOCTRINE

The ascetical path we have thus far described aims to cultivate the unique spiritual aptitude of each individual servant. Therefore, it cannot be set forth as a universal set of rules for all people to follow. In fact, spiritual aptitude varies from servant to servant, and it is shaped by the following factors:

+ the ability to penetrate deeply into prayer and contemplation;
+ consistency in fasting and achieving a lightness of spirit;

+ zeal for worship in the Church and a spiritual understanding of her rites; and

+ diligence in casting off the burden of the flesh and in controlling the desires and impulses from within, so that one may walk by the guidance of the Holy Spirit.

This variety of spiritual aptitudes makes the doctrinal formation of church servants vitally important. For when a servant's ascetical life proceeds along sound theological lines, it is safeguarded against drifting away from the right path, and it resists the influence of strange ideas. Moreover, it ensures that the differences in spiritual aptitude between servants do not turn into divisions among them, which can throw the ministry into a state of confused disarray and cause the young to take up sides with one servant against another.

If ascetical growth is primarily concerned with enriching the relationship between the individual and God, then doctrinal growth is concerned with enriching the relationship between the individual and the community—the Church, the body of believers in every age. We do not have the space here to lay out the curriculum by which the Christian person must develop his theological understanding; we must leave that task to the instructional manuals and theological books that are available. But we may briefly note the salient features of Christian doctrine that a person serving in the Orthodox Church must attend to.

The first essential feature of Orthodox doctrine is its immersion in patristic thought. The Orthodox Church exceeds the Catholics and Protestants in her enthusiasm for the principles and ways of the Fathers of the Early Church. The Orthodox Church still prays as the Fathers did, without abbreviating or altering her liturgy. And if any sort of alteration was found to be necessary with the passing of time, then such change was always consistent with patristic doctrine. The same applies to fasting, worship, and ascetic practice.

The Orthodox spirit is extremely conservative in handling doctrine, and the Orthodox Church shudders at the prospect of the smallest distortion to her doctrinal deposit. For as the Orthodox Church sees it, truth is truth, and anything else is sheer human error. When any dispute arises concerning the smallest point of doctrine, the final arbiter must always be the writings of the Holy Fathers. Any consensus of thought between the saints, such as Anthony, Athanasius, Cyril, their predecessors, or any like-minded ascetics and theologians of the Early Church, should be sufficient to put to rest even the stormiest doctrinal quarrel. If this principle is ever forgotten, it will be impossible for any council, ecclesiastical authority, or saint to rectify doctrinal error. On the other hand, when it is implemented, this theological principle can reconcile the sharpest differences, heal schisms, unify differing points of view, and perfect our lives.

Therefore, one of the cardinal rules a servant must preserve in his heart is to make the teachings of the apostles and fathers the final measuring stick for his faith and religious activity. This naturally calls for the servant to be well versed in the sayings and lives of the fathers. However, a word of caution: to take a firm grasp of patristic teaching does not mean to take a cold, stiff hold of it for the sake of mere outward appearance. It means rather to be changed by the real, solid, powerful experiences of faith that the fathers themselves underwent, and which they successfully passed on to the Church.

The second essential feature of Orthodox doctrine is distinguishing between the human element and the divine element, not in doctrine only, but in every area of life. We have, on the one hand, Catholicism with its characteristic emphasis on the human element in regard to things such as salvation, the intercession and help of the saints, and even the Incarnation itself. On the other hand, we have Protestantism with its emphasis on the divine element—for example, its concept of salvation that is totally devoid of human effort, being a matter of simple divine assurance, without the need of the saints' intercession. In Orthodoxy, however, we find a very fine and careful balance between the human and the divine. The cooperation and interplay of these two components is essential for our faith, struggle, growth, renewal, intercession, and salvation.

God stays close to us as long as we stay close to Him. He is immediately present to those who call upon Him. If we leave Him, He leaves us; if we search for Him, we find Him. When we honor Him, He honors us, and when we disdain Him, we ourselves shrink in worth. Christ stands at the door and knocks. If we open to Him, He enters, but if we are found too sleepy and inert to pay Him any regard, He passes by. If we ask, He will give us whatever we need, but if we do not ask, He will give us nothing. He is forever willing to open to us the door of mercy when we knock. Under no circumstances would He ever deny us entry once we've decided to return to Him, even after a long period of absence. If we renew our minds through the action of the living Word, every day and hour, we will be transformed into the likeness of Christ in sanctity, in truth, and in the hidden grace that is given by the Holy Spirit. If we understand and accept the way of the fathers and prophets and make our supplications through the prayers of the saints, we receive in ourselves the same divine activity that once animated them. We are infused with the grace that once infused them. Whoever receives a prophet will receive a prophet's reward. "The spirits of the prophets are subject to the prophets" (1 Cor. 14:32). In all these examples, we see an extremely close connection between the human call and the divine answer that truly staggers the mind.

To look at the same concept from a different angle, even if spiritual gifts were found to be so plenteous in a particular person that he was equal to the apostles; even if he succeeded in gaining absolutely full control over the body; even if he struggled till bloodshed against sin—without God's grace, his eventual fall would be certain, and he would be (to use St. Paul's word) disqualified. "I discipline my body and bring *it* into subjection, lest, when I have preached to others, I myself should become disqualified" (1 Cor. 9:27). The concept of spiritual struggle is not a means to prove one's strength, but rather a means to reveal God's grace in one's life. This also staggers the mind! As a matter of fact, everything we do in our daily lives, whether religious or secular, should be adorned with God's grace. Otherwise, obstacles and pitfalls will continually beset us, and we will continue to be tripped up, until we learn the proper balance between reliance on self and reliance on Him.

This balance between the human and divine applies not only to outward acts but also to the inner man. The sense of one's sinfulness enables a person also to sense the presence of grace—that is, as much as we humble ourselves and admit our sins, so much can we be consoled by grace and appreciate the redeeming Blood of Christ. In the same way, the amount of grief we feel as a result of our falling into sin is equaled by the amount of forgiving joy that descends upon us from above. If our sense of grief at sin ever ceases, so will our experience of grace and our trust in Christ's Blood. We will have drifted from the Orthodox way.

Equally, if we try to snatch for ourselves the consolations of grace and the joys of the Spirit without admitting and grieving for our sins, we will drift from the Orthodox way. This conscience of the inner man, which strikes a balance between human weakness and God's divine power, must be the vantage point from which we see everything at every stage of life. During those moments in which we feel immersed in the joy of victory and the happiness of salvation, we must not let escape from our memory those dark nights we passed in the gloom of sin. On the other hand, during those moments in which we feel utterly despondent and buried by low self-esteem, we must remember the sun hidden behind the clouds, the divine joy and comfort that are sure to come flying toward us as beautifully and gracefully as a dove.

The third essential feature of Orthodox doctrine is the balance between ecclesiastical authority and personal freedom; this is particularly important in building the servant's character. Orthodox doctrine takes up a middle ground between the absolutist doctrinal authority of the Catholics and the meager doctrinal authority of the Protestants. Similarly, the individual's personal freedom in Orthodox practice occupies a middle ground between the vanishing personal liberty of the Catholics and the imposing personal liberty of the Protestants.

Ecclesiastical authority in the Coptic Church[8] derives its power, its respect, and its very right to exist from the consent of the Church's members. Since laymen are the most numerous members of the Church, they naturally have the largest vote in choosing a patriarch, bishop, priest, or deacon for ordination. If the people do not freely express their approval of a candidate by the joyous cry *Axios* ("worthy"), then the ordination process must come to a halt. The voiced objection of even a single member is sufficient to halt a candidate's ordination, in which case a full investigation and arbitration of conflicting opinions must take place. But if the objector's reason is found wanting, then that member is to be cut off due to the confusion and unrest he has caused to the Church.

Furthermore, the authority vested in a bishop or patriarch is not considered by the Orthodox to be an extension of the leader's personal authority, which he may wield as a prince of the Church. Rather, it is a grace given by God to be handled by the leader as a wise shepherd and steward, for God is the one true Leader, the good

---

8 This description of the ordination process does not describe the current situation in the Orthodox Church as a whole.

Shepherd, the wisest Steward, and the true Bishop of our souls. The patriarch or bishop is a shepherd keeping the sheep of the Shepherd, a steward of what belongs to his Steward, and an overseer being watched by his Overseer. In truth, the bishop possesses no flock of his own, but rather oversees the flock that belongs to God. He oversees not his own children, but God's children. He supervises not his own servants, but God's servants.

Moreover, a bishop does not rule over the Church but within her. He is not her lord but one of her members, honored by the rest of the membership. He should never work as though he were independent of the Church, but as one actually born of her. When the bishop rules or preaches the word, he does so not by the light of his own knowledge and opinions but by the established rules and criteria of the Church. More importantly, his authority is gained by virtue of the love he receives from his flock, who gladly entrust their souls to his care, because of the faithful service he renders to them. In a sense, ecclesiastical authority originates from the people themselves and also finds its completion in them. And so the most even-handed balance between ecclesiastical authority and individual freedom is struck here.

Therefore, the patriarch or bishop may rely confidently on his authority to rule, because the said authority depends on the love and good will of the people. Likewise, the individual believer may trust and submit to the rule of the bishop as if it proceeded from God Himself, for he is also chosen by God for sanctification. Ecclesiastical authority ought to be an expression of the joint decision made by God and the individual together. The individual believer, then, ought to have no misgivings in accepting the authority of church leaders; and the Orthodox Church stands on this principle. In the final analysis, ecclesiastical authority has no validity except that which comes by way of the free consent of the believers. Not only that, but ecclesiastical authority was originally instituted for the protection and enhancement of personal freedom. The rules and regulations of the Church revolve around one common and vital truth: the Christian person's freedom. The Christian must be able to move freely along the path set out by Christ without any obstacle arising from himself, from others, or from the world—within the God-given boundaries the bishops of the Church have fought so vigorously to protect throughout the ages.

Bearing these considerations in mind, the Christian person in general, and the Christian servant in particular, should realize that he is a vital member of the Church who is personally responsible for the soundness and integrity of its leadership. He also has a responsibility to honor and submit to the ecclesiastical authority. Just as a Christian should use his personal liberty to promote and nurture church leadership, so also should the church leadership promote and nurture the Christian's personal liberty.

The fourth essential feature of Orthodox doctrine is the balance between temporal and eternal duties. Once again, the Orthodox Church's views take up a middle ground between discharging one's duties toward one's earthly homeland and the demands of this temporal life on the one hand, and discharging one's duties toward one's heavenly homeland and the demands of eternal life on the other. At one end of the spectrum, Catholicism has tried to "nationalize" the Kingdom of God by instituting the Vatican as a principality upon earth with national borders, with a pope as head of state, and with ambassadors to represent its political interests in other lands. At the other end of the spectrum, we find Protestantism swallowed up in apocalyptic fervor as it waits in suspense for the sudden breakup and dissolution of the nations, Christ's imminent advent with the simultaneous appearance of God's Kingdom, and the swift rapture of believing souls to heaven.

The Orthodox Church has always stood midway between these two poles by drawing the fine distinction between the kingdom of Caesar and the Kingdom of God: "Render to Caesar the things that are Caesar's, and to God the things that are God's" (Mark 12:17). She has calmly resigned the hour of Christ's coming to the province of God's counsel (as the Lord requested), and she has exhorted her children to work and serve honestly under the worldly authorities, whoever they may be—Christian, Muslim, or heathen. At the same time, she has continued to serve and worship in deserts, caves, and mountains and to discharge her higher and more sacred duties toward God's Kingdom that is to come.

Thus, Orthodoxy has become the world's tutor in worship, sacrifice, and self-transcendence. Even more, as long as Orthodoxy securely holds to its original belief in the vain and ephemeral nature of the world, its children will paradoxically remain better citizens and more responsible members of their earthly homeland than are the worldly themselves. Their rule and standard will be the biblical precept, "Do not lay up for yourselves treasures on earth . . . but lay up for yourselves treasures in heaven" (Matt. 6:19, 20).

"For our citizenship is in heaven, from which we also eagerly wait for the Savior, the Lord Jesus Christ" (Phil. 3:20). "For here we have no continuing city, but we seek the one to come" (Heb. 13:14). This sentiment of the Early Church is also aptly expressed in the Epistle to Diognetus: "They dwell in their own countries, but simply as sojourners. As citizens, they share in all things with others, and yet endure all things as if foreigners. Every foreign land is to them as their native country, and every land of their birth as a land of strangers."

The secret to this delicate balance in fulfilling one's obligations to both one's earthly and heavenly countries is to be found in the sublime levels of asceticism and transcendence achieved by the Fathers.

Through them, the truths and joys of the Eternal Kingdom were communicated to the Church. They lived in the Kingdom to come as they walked on the earth, and they enjoyed it to the full while still carrying out their daily tasks here on earth. They charted a path for the Church in the midst of the duties and obligations of the world, and they lived the "last things" while struggling in the present. They passed through this life shouldering the hardships of the flesh, while their faces bore the smile of victory and beamed the joys of the coming age.

We hope that this brief summary has shone a clear light on the salient points of Orthodox doctrine, so that they may be used by the servants and leaders of the Church for building up the doctrinal stature of those they serve and for plumbing the magnificent depths of Orthodoxy.

3
CHARACTER BUILDING

When we speak of character, we must begin by asking ourselves an essential question: How do good character and conduct fit into the scheme of Christianity? Is character the central preoccupation of the faith, and is good conduct the heart of Christ's message? The answer is no, for the goal of faith is eternal life, and the heart of Christ's message is Christ Himself. We are to live with Him and for Him, for He is the eternal life and Eternal Kingdom we seek: "I am the way . . . and the life" (John 14:6). Therefore, what is the source of good character, and what is the final aim of correct conduct in the Christian scheme?

Character is the task of the soul in the same way that vision is the task of the eyes. If the eyes are in good health and function in the presence of light, they will produce good vision. If the soul is in good health and lives in the presence of Christ, it will produce good character. Good character, in other words, is the fruit of a Christian life. Consequently, it is impossible for a Christian to contemplate or pursue good character apart from Christ. Christ Himself is the secret to good character as well as the source of correct conduct.

The definition of character in Christian theology, then, is not simply a list of virtues that includes honesty, decency, trustworthiness, integrity, and the rest, but rather it goes above all these. To "have character" as a Christian means rather to bear the character of Christ Himself. Virtues like honesty and decency are, from a worldly point of view, simply traits meant to facilitate a successful and pleasurable life on earth. But honesty and trustworthiness, from the Christian point of view, are directly connected to the concerns of eternal life. They are not intended to secure a stable life here on earth so much as to ensure the Christian's safe passage through this world on his way to the eternal.

The worldly man is, at best, honest and trustworthy simply out of respect for his personal relationships, or to create a good reputation, or for business reasons. The Christian, on the other hand, is trustworthy (even in the smallest things) not because he has his eye on anything in the world, but because he has his eyes set on something much greater—heaven. The Christian, in fact, performs his work with a diligence and trustworthiness that outstrip the requirements of the work itself, because his diligence does not flow from a personal ambition to see the work succeed. His diligence is rather a result of his seeking a reward greater than this world and a life greater than that which is fed by food and drink. "Whatever you do, do it heartily, as to the Lord and not to men" (Col. 3:23). Therefore, the diligence and honesty of the Christian can never be twisted by blackmail or human failure. They can never be stopped, even by the threat of death or the deprivation of pleasure. For this type of character is not of this world; its force and resilience far surpass the mundane virtues required for life on earth.

And so the task of Christian character is to transform the human soul from a life according to the flesh to a life according to the spirit. This is essentially the mission of the Christian servant. Since his life-long work involves progressing, together with those he serves, from a fleshly life to a spiritual one, the Christian understanding of character becomes a standard by which to judge his every word and deed, whether in service, family life, or work life.

In order to clearly delineate what are the distinct qualities of Christian virtue, we must first carefully distinguish it from merely human virtue. From a worldly point of view, human character excels in its ability to compromise between the demands of the flesh and the philosophy of the mind, between present reality and future expectations, between emotion and judgment, between feeling and thought, between personal needs and the needs of others. From the Christian point of view, on the contrary, Christian character excels in contrasting between this life and the next. It sees a clear strife between the demands of the flesh and the demands of the spirit. It perceives an antithetical tension between the blessings of the world and the blessings of heaven, between pleasing people and pleasing God.

Human virtue effects a sort of truce between a person and himself, between himself and contemporary life, and between himself and others. Christian virtue, on the contrary, starts out by pitting a person against himself, against contemporary life, and against others, but its finished work results in a *harmony between* the person and everything around him. "If anyone comes to Me and does not hate his father and mother, wife and children, brothers and sisters, yes, and his own life also, he cannot be My disciple" (Luke 14:26). Indeed, it is a marvelous thing that though Christian virtue initially requires strife between a Christian and his environment, its end result is a peaceful concord between the two. This is a reflection of the Christian's walk on the path to salvation, because it means that he has begun to extricate himself from selfishness, worldly ambition, and egotistical pride—in short, all those flaws that contaminate a person's character, which ordinary human virtue cannot defeat, no matter how hard it tries.

Here is a paradox. When a Christian clings tenaciously to truth and uprightness and resists self-conceit, the ambitions of the modern world, and the urge to trample other people underfoot, he will be immediately lifted to a plane far above himself, above the modern world, and above other people. He will rise, in other words, to the plane where God and eternal life are found. Once that is achieved, he will naturally return to himself, but without conceit. He will return to the modern world, but without ambition. He will return to others, but without rivalry and competition. Christian character, in this sense, does not merely consist in a mixed bag of virtues, but it is the very road to heaven, a road the Christian may rely on to lead him through the worst trials and bring him to his desired destination.

We begin to see more clearly, now, the vast difference between these two types of character. Natural human character (even in its best manifestations) cooperates with one's desires, the world's demands, and the opinion of other people. Christian virtue, however, challenges one's desires, the world's demands, and the opinions of others. While natural human virtue claims as its objective the promotion of general human welfare on earth, it does this by draining the spiritual thirst of the human soul and devaluing its hunger for God. Thus, it cheapens the life of man as being a thing of little substance. "Character" then becomes a phantom quality that serves only to make human life more efficient or more proper in appearance. It ends in being just a theatrical act that people put on until the curtain drops and the performance is ended.

But because of Christian virtue's unique interaction with the ego and the world, it is able to lift the human soul from the base, paltry level of efficiency or productivity to a far higher state of being. It makes integrity in work a greater thing than the work itself; it makes diligence a greater thing than success itself; it makes honesty a greater thing than the friendship itself; and it makes justice more important than a group's collective agreement. Christian character thus leads us to the highest plane of humanity. The noble pursuits of this world—art, literature, politics, education, psychology, physical exercise—are, without a Christian spirit, nothing more than hazy and unsure guides to the soul of man. However, when art, literature, education, and the other pursuits are imbued with a Christian spirit, they are emptied of their self-centered and competitive nature, and they become conduits of good things like love, sacrifice, and goodwill. Only then can man be loosed from his attachment to base things like money and rise to the wonderful spiritual heights for which he has always pined.

After this short introduction to the idea of Christian character, we must ask an important question. Is Christian character a law? In other words, is it obligatory? To answer this, we must remember that Christianity imparts a new nature to man, far more exalted than this sickly natural one. Man's nature clings to its original creative purpose, which is union with God and eternal life with Him. Now, when man fell, he was deprived of this eternal life. In order to elevate his animal nature and protect him from drifting too far afield, God made him subject to certain laws and obligatory ordinances (see Ex. 20:1–17):

+ You shall have no other god besides Me.
+ You shall love the Lord your God with all your heart.

- You shall love your neighbor as yourself.
- You shall honor your father and mother.
- You shall not murder.
- You shall not steal.
- You shall not commit adultery.
- You shall not take the name of the Lord your God in vain.
- You shall not bear false witness.
- You shall not covet.

Christ then came and granted us a new birth, which endowed us with a new, spiritual, exalted nature. Through this new nature, God gave us that eternal life that He had originally given us, but which we had carelessly squandered. In doing this, He delivered us from the severe demands of fixed ordinances. In fact, He abrogated the entire Law itself: "Therefore the law was our tutor *to bring us* to Christ, that we might be justified by faith. But after faith has come, we are no longer under a tutor" (Gal. 3:24, 25). The laws and commandments of the Old Covenant were spiritual in nature, and so they could never be reconciled to our fallen sinful nature. As a result, they became a mere punitive code to judge us severely when we erred. But now we live in newness of life, in the power of the Resurrection, in a mystical Kingdom buried deep within the heart. And so we no longer live under a penal code that judges us for our character flaws; rather, we live with God by virtue of Christ's own perfect character. We have been given the mind of Christ, the obedience of Christ, and His very Spirit. These traits of the new nature together compose "Christian character."

Christian character, then, is not a law. It is not a thing imposed on us from above. It is rather a beloved and desirable nature that unites with our soul; it agrees with our desire for heaven; it complements our new man. Our union with Christ has stripped the penal code of its authority and sway over man; indeed, it has been emptied of its very substance. The Law that was originally given to train our animal nature is not suited to train our souls: "That which is born of the flesh is flesh, and that which is born of the Spirit is spirit" (John 3:6). Our love for Christ has caused us to advance beyond the law against murder to a law against anger, and we rise above the law against anger to obey the command to love our enemies. The transformation of the Law is the result of a transformation in our own nature. The punitive code breaks down and dissolves under the fervent, explosive love we possess in Christ.

The love of Christ in us has rendered honesty and transparency in everything we do a matter of course. Again, Christian character is not an obligatory law that a person must strive to fulfill, but a description of the new nature of man. It is his greatest joy. It exudes love in every condition. It is the mysterious work of Christ in the heart of the person who has been born of the Spirit. It is the luminous wings given by the Holy Spirit to a person for his ascent from earth to heaven.

The next essential question, then, is how to build a person's Christian character. Is it done by observing rules, performing exercises, and receiving rewards and punishments? Such an approach will not work, for it is directed solely to the natural man, and it develops qualities of the soul that are natural and customary. Rules, exercises, rewards, and punishments do indeed improve the quality and conduct of human nature; however, they are incapable of raising a person above his own nature.

A circus tamer must resort to rewarding and punishing his animals to maximize the intelligence and skills they have by nature; however, the trainer is in no way able to create new skills that are foreign to their animal nature, such as speech or laughter. The unique traits of Christian character were not placed in man's original nature, for they are spiritual in nature and cannot be acquired or increased by the usual educational methods. They are not skills but gifts—truth, honesty, faithfulness, sincere love, and so on. Such gifts are given by the Spirit and increase in the Spirit, transforming human nature by the Spirit.

There is no way Christian character can be planted and grow in a person without constant communion with Christ through prayer and love. Therefore, we must surrender our hearts and minds to the direction of the Spirit, for the Spirit takes what is Christ's and gives it to us. The servant acquires truth by tasting Christ's truth, which then enters into his veins and takes up its abode in his heart. The servant acquires faithfulness when he experiences Christ's faithfulness, which then sinks into his innermost being and stamps itself on all his members. The servant acquires wholeness and integrity when Christ reigns over his entire being.

4
POINTERS FOR EXPERIENCING SPIRITUAL LIFE

Everything we have said regarding the psychological and spiritual edification of the servant was meant to set the stage for discussing Orthodox spiritual experience. Spiritual experience, as it has been described by the Church and her saints, is powered by the new life granted to man. Here are several specific attributes required for spiritual experience:

+ A sense of God's real presence
+ An overflowing joy in the heart for God's word that makes a person constantly hungry for more
+ A firm trust in God's promises that creates an imperishable hope
+ A personal familiarity with the Person of Christ, as a faithful friend who inspires a deep love in the heart

+ A zealous conviction to be Christ's witness, even without any formal training, and readiness (if necessary) for martyrdom
+ A certainty of the Holy Spirit's indwelling, and a sharp awareness of His guidance
+ Constant self-judgment and identification of personal sins

Unfortunately, these spiritual attributes cannot be systematized or otherwise arranged into a formal catalogue. They are mystical actions that lead to profound spiritual experiences, and as such, cannot be explained with mere words. Even if we strained our minds to their utmost capacity to define these characteristics, our attempted explanations would certainly fall short. The most our words can do is to list them and to provoke the heart to seek and pursue them. The important question still remains: how does a person taste genuine spiritual experiences? The answer is to be found in the soul's relationship with the Holy Spirit. Let us offer now a few pointers for achieving such spiritual experience.

1. Be Free of the Influence of the World

It must be clarified that the aforementioned attributes are not the offspring of religious "feeling" or the product of religious "exercise." They are rather our way, truth, and life. They are our way in that they correct our footsteps if they happen to be moving too fast along the broad street of the world. They are our truth to correct us if our souls happen to be too attached to the famous heroes of the world. They are our life, whose light cannot illuminate us if we have satisfied ourselves with the life and glory of the world.

It must be quite clear from what we have said that achieving spiritual experience requires first of all a struggle against the world; it also follows that gaining access to real spiritual experience hinges on our inner detachment from attraction to the world. This detachment, this liberation, in turn depends on our cooperation with God's

Spirit in the daily and hourly struggles against the world's deviant ways, its false honors and heroes.

St. Macarius comments on the issue of spiritual experience with words that are pregnant with wisdom: "Those souls whose love for God is constant and unflagging are worthy of eternal life. They will strive for independence from earthly lusts and will enter into that mystical and ineffable union with the Holy Spirit which brings a fullness of grace [spiritual experience]." Conversely, souls that have been deceived by their obsession with the flesh do not even think to seek after holiness. They seem to have no interest in receiving the Spirit of consolation (the Paraclete), neither do they ask for clearer vision, or spiritual fullness, or perfection. Thus, they are not given the strength to resist carnal desires. Similar to these are those souls who initially were found worthy to receive grace but who lost it through negligence and carelessness. So the experience of spiritual life begins with love for God, requires resistance to carnal desire, and ends, according to that beautifully phrased description of St. Macarius, in "a mystical and ineffable union with the Holy Spirit which brings a fullness of grace."

2. Be Devoted to Christ

Christ requests, indeed requires, each of His followers to determine, before anything else, the nature of their relationship with Him. Consider the following:

"Do you love Me?"—thrice repeated (John 21:15–17).

"Sell everything you have . . . and come, follow Me" (Luke 18:22).

"Jesus said to him, 'Let the dead bury their own dead, but you go and preach the kingdom of God'" (Luke 9:60).

"He who loves father or mother more than Me is not worthy of Me. And he who loves son or daughter more than Me is not worthy of Me" (Matt. 10:37).

"If anyone comes to Me and does not hate his father and mother, wife and children, brothers and sisters, yes, and his own life also, he cannot be My disciple" (Luke 14:26).

"If you love Me, keep My commandments" (John 14:15).

"Could you not watch [with Me] one hour?" (Mark 14:37).

"Then He said to the disciple, 'Behold your mother!'" (John 19:27).

Christ requires us to clarify the nature of our relationship to Him, so that we can enter by Him and with Him into the power and truth of the salvation we seek. The words of Christ cited above indicate that He is not pleased with any sort of relationship that does not rise above all other relationships we have with people and that does not rank higher in importance than every other preoccupation in this world. "For what profit is it to a man if he gains the whole world, and loses his own soul?" (Matt. 16:26).

Indeed, this is the positive aspect that complements the negative aspect of achieving liberation, which we have described above. By ranking Christ above every person and preoccupation in our life, even above life itself, we will be automatically rewarded with the truth that "sets us free" (see John 8:32). First, we struggle with God's help against the world, its lusts, the flesh, and every carnal yoke; then we elevate Christ in our lives above everybody and everything to receive that inherent power of truth that helps us overcome every harmful thing. The question that faces us then is this: Which of the two steps is more important? Does the difficulty necessarily precede the reward? Indeed, the two are intertwined, beginning together and finishing their work together.

It must be clear to the reader that defining the nature of our relationship with Christ allows us to receive strength and to reach the way of truth by the shortest and quickest means. The knowledge of the truth that is in Christ does not lead to mere hypothetical gifts, such as a gift of oratory, but provides one with an active, tangible strength. It is a liberating power that uses its authority to empower our mind, will, deeds, habits, and our very nature. The power we gain through our relationship with Christ is the power of life, the fullness of eternal life that taunts and defies death.

The power to face death that the martyrs received by virtue of their love and knowledge of Christ was unrecognized by their torturers, who had no idea that the truth that abided in the martyrs released them from the burdens of this world and from the fear of death. Their blood witnessed to the genuine nature of their spiritual experience. Our relationship to Christ is what determines our worthiness to receive spiritual experiences.

3. Be Prepared to Meet God

Spiritual experience means entering God's presence. Are we ready to face Him?

We may have a desire to meet with Him and to converse with Him. We may even have boldly pleaded to receive a vision of Him. The question remains: how ready are we to receive such a great presence, conversation, or vision? Three qualities are required in a person before he can see God.

The first quality is a simple heart. In the spiritual life, a simple heart means believing the unbelievable; it means faith in the impossible; it means confidence in things unseen. It follows that a skeptical attitude, a rigidly logical mind, and a cowardly will are all massive obstacles on the road to spiritual experience.

The second quality is the ability to transcend circumstances and to see through appearances. One must remember that God can be found in all the circumstances and passages of life. If we are not as prepared to meet Him in our griefs and pains as we are in our joys and successes, then our spiritual experience will remain shaky and eventually fade away. Once we have entered into a conversation with

God, no other message or communication (no matter how critical) can interfere with it. Once we have received the vision of God, no other sight (no matter how attractive) can erase it from our heart and memory.

The third quality is the preparedness to receive God through others. "He who receives you receives Me" (Matt. 10:40). "Assuredly, I say to you, inasmuch as you did *it* to one of the least of these My brethren, you did *it* to Me" (Matt. 25:40). One of the absolute necessities of real spiritual life is the heart's readiness to see God in a suffering brother or sister, in a hungry orphan, in a poor needy widow, in the sick, in the downtrodden, in the homeless man, in the stranger, in the indigent, in the persecuted, in the victim of injustice—in short, in every single human being without prejudice.

To that end, Christ—who is the express image of God—desired to make these poor souls an image of Himself. He decreed that the acceptance of Himself, and the acceptance of God, was contingent on one's willingness to serve such sick and needful souls. Such service is the quickest and shortest path to true spiritual experience. These weak and suffering members of Christ's Body (crucified for the world) must have a unique prominence in our eyes if we desire to be privileged with a vision of the glorified Christ.

> "Then the righteous will answer Him, saying, 'Lord, when did we see You hungry and feed *You*, or thirsty and give *You* drink? When did we see You a stranger and take *You* in, or naked and clothe *You*? Or when did we see You sick, or in prison, and come to You?' And the King will answer and say to them, 'Assuredly, I say to you, inasmuch as you did *it* to one of the least of these My brethren, you did *it* to Me.'" (Matt. 25:37–40)

4. Be Prepared to Witness to the Truth

It is an acknowledged truth that one's entry into the life of spiritual experience is equivalent to one's entry into the truth. The truth in this sense is the fullness and power of the new life given to us by Christ. Being born into this natural world imposes certain duties on a person, one of which (the primary one, in fact) is to protect this natural life against all forces that try to destroy it. The same is true of being born into the eternal life. If one wishes to receive the divine truth that is the gift of spiritual life, the first duty is to be ready to witness to the truth. This witness is twofold: first, it is opposed to everything that disparages the truth; second, it is attracted to every soul that desires to receive the truth.

Thus, spiritual experiences come seldom to the person who is unwilling to oppose evil. The sayings of spiritual life become offensive to those who are unwilling to hear the testimony of the Gospel: "For we cannot but speak the things which we have seen and heard" (Acts 4:20). Witnessing in this sense is not an obligation or stipulation placed on the believer, as though it were a special kind of virtue or a way to please God. Rather, it is the natural outflowing of a person whose life abides in the truth, or in whose life the truth abides. Thus, one's inner readiness to be a witness to the truth—with all the heart, mind, strength, and will—is a requirement for having spiritual experiences.

The ranks of the Early Church were bursting with countless numbers of martyrs whose endurance confounded philosophers, governors, and judges. They amazed these great figures by their wisdom and prudence, by the strength they had to crucify their wills, together with their meekness, as of lambs. These were the fruits of their spiritual experiences, the result of their relationship with Christ.

Ancient Faith Publishing hopes you have enjoyed and benefited from this book. The proceeds from the sales of our books only partially cover the costs of operating our nonprofit ministry—which includes both the work of **Ancient Faith Publishing** and the work of **Ancient Faith Radio**. Your financial support makes it possible to continue this ministry both in print and online. Donations are tax-deductible and can be made at **www.ancientfaith.com**.

To view our other publications,
please visit our website: **store.ancientfaith.com**

 **ANCIENT FAITH RADIO**

Bringing you Orthodox Christian music, readings,
prayers, teaching, and podcasts 24 hours a day since 2004 at
ancientfaith.com